THE HISTORY AND TECHNIQUES
OF THE GREAT MASTERS

WHISTLER

THE HISTORY AND TECHNIQUES
OF THE GREAT MASTERS

WHISTLER

Michael Howard

CHARTWELL
BOOKS, INC.

A QUARTO BOOK

Published by Chartwell Books
A Division of Book Sales, Inc.
110 Enterprise Avenue
Secaucus, New Jersey 07094

ISBN 1-55521-496-7

This book was designed and produced by
Quarto Publishing plc
The Old Brewery, 6 Blundell Street
London N7 9BH

Project Editor Hazel Harrison
Designer Carol Perks
Picture Researcher Liz Somerville

Art Director Moira Clinch
Editorial Director Carolyn King

Typeset by Aptimage Limited
22 Clinton Place, Seaford, East Sussex BN25 1NP
Manufactured in Hong Kong by Regent
Publishing Services Limited
Printed in Hong Kong by Leefung-Asco
Printers Ltd

CONTENTS

INTRODUCTION

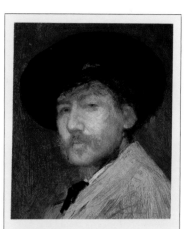

JAMES MCNEILL WHISTLER
*Arrangement in Gray: Portrait
of the Painter*
(detail)
1872-73, Detroit Institute of Art

The words of a contemporary neatly encapsulate the self-projected image of James Abbott McNeill Whistler as one of the major eccentrics of his time. "A prince among men . . . he wore a short black coat, white vest, white ducks and pumps; a low collar and a slim black tie, carefully arranged with one long end crossing his vest." Whistler's brilliant wit, exquisite taste and tetchy rivalry with Oscar Wilde are part of folklore, but his place in the history of art is less easy to assess. Writers, critics and even fellow artists have regarded him as an outsider, a fugitive from tradition, never quite able to find a home among the many avant-garde factions of his day. His life and art present us with a tangle of paradoxes, and the very flamboyance of his personality has always tended to overshadow a real appreciation of his very remarkable work.

Possibly the only great artist to attend West Point Military Academy, Whistler was born in 1834 in Lowell, Massachusetts. He spent a substantial part of his childhood, however, in St Petersburg, Russia, where his father, a civil engineer, was employed by Czar Nicholas I to supervise the development of the St Petersburg-Moscow railway. In 1849 Whistler's father died unexpectedly, bringing to an end the family's affluent ex-patriate lifestyle, and they returned to America. The young Whistler bowed to his mother's wishes and enrolled at West Point in 1851, but his commitment to a military career was less than total; he later remarked of his (probably deliberate) failure to complete his studies, "If silicon had been a gas, I'd have been a Major-General."

Student years in Paris
He then spent a year as a cartographer in the US Coastal Survey Office in Washington, where he gained a sound introduction to the techniques of etching. But he was drawn to the Bohemian life, particularly after reading Henri Mürger's colorful novel, *La Vie de Bohème* (1848), and in 1855 he left for Paris, never to return to the land of

his birth. There he became friendly with other artists, notably Gustave Courbet and later Edgar Degas and Henri Fantin-Latour, and after six months he enrolled at the Académie Gleyre, where several of the painters later to become the Impressionists also studied. Charles Gleyre specialized in the popular Neo-Grecian style which drew on antique subject matter, both as a pretext for displaying the skill of the artist and as an acceptable means of introducing an erotic element into paintings. Gleyre's studio maxims, such as "Black is the basis of all" and "Style is everything," were famous, and his influence on Whistler's subsequent painting was stronger than is often acknowledged.

Although the young Whistler did not neglect his studies, he was satirized as the "idle apprentice" in the novel *Trilby* by George du Maurier, who was in Paris at the same time. In the book, Whistler featured as one Jos. Sibley, whose lazy southern ways, outlandish dress and self-consciously idiosyncratic behavior set him apart from the rest of the "Paris Gang," which included the subsequent President of the Royal Academy, Edward Poynter. (Whistler quite rightly objected to his portrayal in the serialization that ran in *Harper's Monthly Magazine*, and after the inevitable lawsuit, references to him in future editions of the book were excised.)

Formative years: the 1860s
Whistler's first major canvas, *At the Piano*, was rejected by the Paris Salon of 1859 and, following its acceptance and success at the Royal Academy the following year, he decided to move to London, where he felt he had a better chance of artistic and financial success. This was a period of transition and experimentation in the arts, and Whistler's work of the 1860s reflects elements of the new concerns shared by the avant-garde at the time, as well as revealing the twin influences of Courbet and the pre-Raphaelites. Gustave Courbet, the leading painter in the Realist movement, which took everyday life as its subject

JAMES MCNEILL WHISTLER
Symphony in White No. 1: The White Girl
1862, National Gallery of Art, Washington

Whistler has left us his own description of this painting. His mistress and model Jo is seen "standing against a window which filters the light through a transparent white muslin curtain, but the figure receives a strong light from the right, and therefore the picture, barring the red hair, is one gorgeous mass of brilliant white." Despite the artist's subsequent reworking of the canvas, notably the face, hands, wolfskin and carpet, his description still holds true.

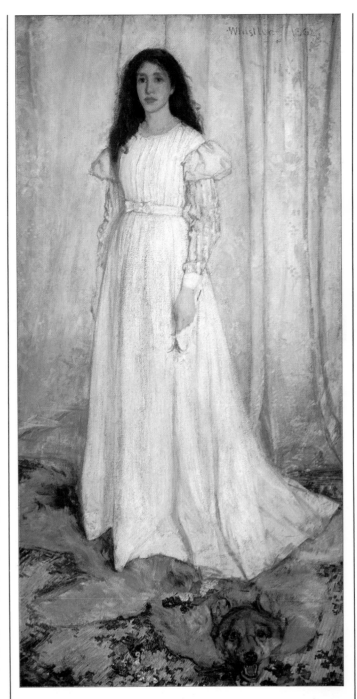

matter, was admired by all the young painters who were seeking a new direction for art. Whistler's contact with the pre-Raphaelite painters, especially Millais and Rossetti, encouraged him in his belief that the fundamental purpose of art was the creation of beauty. Velasquez, whose work he had seen at the Manchester Art Treasures Exhibition in 1857, was to provide a lasting influence, and his presence can be felt in all Whistler's work throughout his career.

In 1862 he painted the *White Girl* which, like his earlier work, *Wapping* (see page 22), featured Jo, his Irish model. The painting was rejected by the Academy, and Whistler, enraged, sent it to the Paris Salon of 1863. The French jury that year refused over 4000 works, and such was the outcry from the rejected artists that the Emperor Napoleon III instituted a Salon des Refusés, where Whistler's picture shared a *succès de scandale* with Edouard Manet's innovatory canvas, *Déjeuner sur l'herbe.*

Whistler's painting, like the *Little White Girl* of the following year (see page 26), illustrates his concern to minimize the narrative implications of his subject matter, his unusual use — or non-use — of color and his penchant for pre-Raphaelite images of dreaming women. As the decade progressed the solid Realist characteristics of Courbet's art became increasingly modified by the influence of Rossetti and Millais.

After a number of years of crossing and re-crossing the Channel, Whistler eventually settled down in London — although the word "settled" is not entirely appropriate to one for whom permanence could never be more than a relative state — and in so doing he decided his fate. Had he remained in France with friends and colleagues such as Degas (to whom he later gave a copy of his collected writings, *The Gentle Art of Making Enemies*) his art and his place in the art history books would have been very different. Not only had he rejected the heritage of Courbet's Realism, he had also cut himself off from immediate contact with progressive Parisian art. It is possible that he might have found the competition from the French capital too daunting; he was always very uncertain of his own technical prowess.

In 1865 Whistler came into contact with the work of the English painter Albert Moore, whose languid and harmonious paintings of women in Greek dress exerted a profound effect upon him. Japanese prints had already begun to make a strong impact on painting, and now Whistler saw the arts of Greece and Japan as the cornerstones of his theory of a new art based on the twin qualities of harmony and beauty. "It seems to me," he wrote to Fantin-Latour in 1868, "that color ought to be, as it were, embroidered on the canvas, that is to say, the same color ought to appear continually here and there, in the same way that a thread appears in an embroidery . . . In this way, the whole will form a harmony. Look how well the Japanese understood this. They never look for contrast, on the contrary they're after repetition." Whistler was one of the first collectors of Oriental artefacts, but his attempt to assimilate Japanese prints into his work led to a series of uneasy paintings in which the various elements vied with each other in canvases that sought a modernity very different from that of Courbet's earthy Realism.

Toward the middle of the decade Whistler adopted Albert Moore's practice of signing his paintings with a symbol instead of his name, and the one he chose was a butterfly, developed from his own initials and drawn in the Japanese manner. Millais also used a distinctive monogram, and Moore himself signed his work with a scallop shell motif. Aubrey Beardsley was later to use a three-stemmed candlestick as his signifier, by way of homage to Whistler.

Painting and music

In 1867 Whistler painted a picture of two girls dressed in white, placed in an all-white setting, and entitled it *Symphony in White No. 3*. This was his first use of a

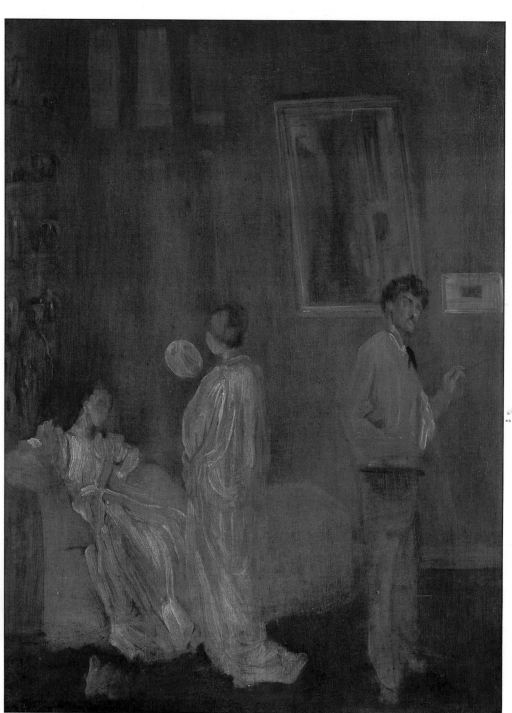

JAMES MCNEILL WHISTLER
The Artist's Studio
c1865, Municipal Gallery of
Modern Art, Dublin

Whistler intended to paint a monumental canvas for the Paris Salon of 1866 featuring his friends Albert Moore and Henri Fantin-Latour in his own studio. His ambition was to produce a work equal to Courbet's *The Artist's Studio* and Fantin's two group portraits (one of which features Whistler). But this was never realized, and all that remains of his idea are two modest-sized sketches, of which this painting is one.

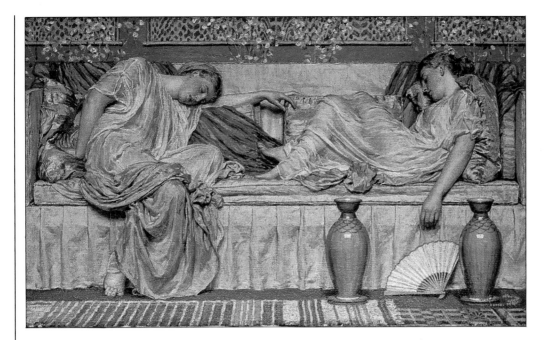

ALBERT MOORE
Beads
c 1875, National Gallery of
Scotland, Edinburgh

Albert Moore's work, stressing the formal arrangement of pictorial elements, had a great influence upon Whistler, and foreshadows the well-known dictum of the French symbolist painter Maurice Denis. Denis wrote in 1890 that "a picture, before being a battle horse, a nude woman, or some anecdote, is essentially a flat surface covered with colors assembled in a certain order."

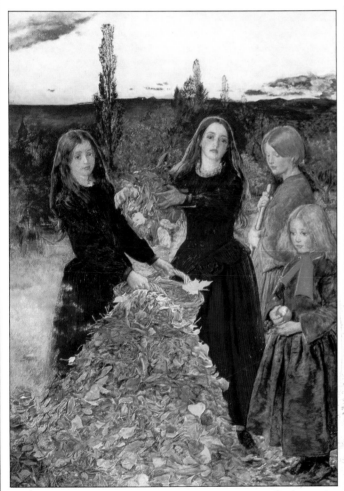

JOHN EVERETT MILLAIS
Autumn Leaves
1856, Manchester City Art
Gallery

Whistler was very impressed with Millais' early work, drawn to its powerful symbolic content and evocative use of color to convey a sense of moody melancholy. A subtle erotic element which underpins much of the pre-Raphaelites' work also appears in Whistler's paintings.

musical term to highlight a picture's abstract qualities, a practice that would last until the end of his life (the earlier paintings were re-titled accordingly). Many of his paintings were called "arrangements" or "harmonies," and his views of the Thames were "nocturnes," a term borrowed from Chopin and suggested by one of Whistler's patrons, Sir Francis Leyland. The parallel between painting and music was one of the major debates among members of the avant-garde at the time, and Whistler's titles stress the musical analogies he tried to evoke in the mind of the viewer.

In the 1870s Whistler "came of age" as a painter; he finally threw off the influence of Courbet, abandoned the depictions of antique luxury suggested by Moore's classicism, and returned to the themes of the city and the river, producing many of the works for which he is best known today. The opaque paint surface, rich detail and human interest of his earlier paintings, such as *Wapping*, were replaced by a number of relatively small works in which a thin translucent wash of paint was used to evoke the atmosphere of London, and particularly the river, seen by night and transposed into a series of harmonious relationships of line, color and form. There is no moral or social element in Whistler's work — he did not consider comment or criticism to be the goal of art. Mundane reality, in his view, should be studied only in order to be transformed by the artist's vision into something possessing both flawless beauty and universal significance.

The society portrait painter
By this time Whistler was beginning to make his mark as a portrait painter, although his extreme perfectionism in every project he undertook resulted in a relatively small

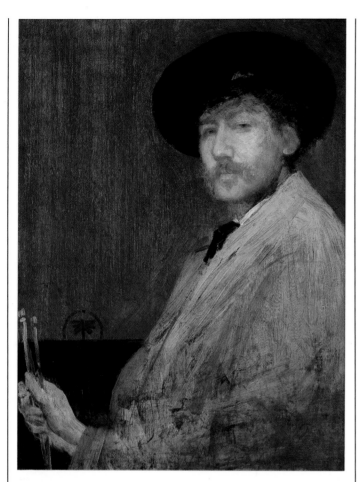

JAMES MCNEILL WHISTLER
*Arrangement in Gray: Portrait
of the Painter*
1872-73, Detroit Institute of
Art

Titian and Rembrandt were
very important to Whistler,
and this self-portrait contains
elements from the work of

both masters. It is the first
portrait to feature his famous
single lock of white hair.
Whistler has scraped down the
jacket area, which has led to
an odd visual ambiguity: is it
the artist's left or right hand
that grasps the paintbrush?

number of surviving paintings. He made intolerable demands on his sitters; poor Miss Cicely Alexander (see page 46) had to endure over seventy sessions before Whistler pronounced himself happy with the result. Every element associated with his creations had to be exquisite in conception and appearance, and Whistler planned each painting to have only a single skin, or surface, of paint, which meant that every one must, in effect, be completed in a single session. In practice, this involved a continued series of separate attempts to produce the ideal work, since each time a painting fell short of the artist's own high standards it would be scraped down and begun afresh at another sitting, instead of being corrected and reworked in the conventional way. When successful, as in the portrait of Miss Cicely Alexander, this approach has a freshness and a

unity of surface that is comparable to Velasquez, whose paintings Whistler always hoped to equal.

The artist as interior designer

Following pre-Raphaelite practice, Whistler designed his own frames, which were invariably simple, often arrangements of fine reeds, painted with a variety of Japanese-inspired motifs in various shades of gold. As a picture should be a perfect piece of decoration on a wall, it was inevitable that he should treat the frame as a means of continuing and refining the decorative aspects of the painting, and the logical extension to this was to take his principles of design into the environment itself. Most of his ventures into the area of interior design have sadly long since vanished, although Claude Monet's house at Giverny may well have been inspired by Whistler's ideas. His reputation as an interior designer of genius must rest on the reconstruction by Washington's Freer Gallery of his Peacock Room.

In 1876 Sir Francis Leyland commissioned the artist to make some minor alterations to his dining room, which housed a collection of porcelain and Whistler's portrait of Christine Spartali of 1864. The result was one of the most famous interiors of the 19th century. Essentially, Whistler got carried away. Instead of merely repainting the small red flowers on the priceless 16th-century hand-tooled leather that covered the walls of Leyland's room, he obliterated it with blue paint on which he introduced swaggering blue peacocks, which strut about their blue-green and gold enclosures quivering with pride. A priceless Persian carpet with a red border which he saw as clashing with the new color scheme was trimmed to remove the offending red, and poor Leyland returned home to find that not only had his walls been completely overpainted without his permission, but that his private residence had been the stamping ground of Whistler's entourage throughout that winter. He never forgave Whistler this infringement of his privacy — nor did he appreciate the artist's close relationship with his wife — and accordingly withdrew his hitherto generous support of the artist and paid only half of his bill for 2000 guineas.

The artist versus the establishment

Whistler's relationship with the British art establishment had never been a happy one, and it reached breaking point in 1877 when John Ruskin made a disparaging reference to Whistler's painting of *The Falling Rocket* (see page 54), exhibited at the opening exhibition of the Grosvenor Gallery. Ruskin wrote that he had "seen, and heard, much of Cockney impudence before now; but never expected to hear a coxcomb ask 200 guineas for flinging a pot of paint in the public's face." Although Ruskin was by now an old man, he was still the most respected and feared of all Victorian critics, and Whistler was forced into an attempt to protect his reputation, and hence his portrait practice. He sued Ruskin for libel. The case was a farce and the result of the court action was public humiliation — technically, Whistler won but was awarded a derisory farthing, the smallest coin in British currency at the time — for damages.

The artist, already impoverished by Leyland's withdrawal of support, was declared bankrupt, and he still had to pay his legal costs. With characteristic aplomb, he hung the farthing from his watch fob and set out to recoup his losses, turning again to etching in which he had always enjoyed both popular and critical acclaim and which could be considered as a sound commercial enterprise. He left England for Venice, where he stayed

from 1879 to 1880, and produced a series of etchings and pastels of the city, seeking out moody subjects and unfamiliar corners. He had earlier used his skill in etching to capture the bustle of London's dockside in sharp-focused detail in his justly famous *Thames Set* of 1859, but now he exploited the medium in a different way, producing evocations rather than literal descriptions.

JAMES MCNEILL WHISTLER
Harmony in Blue and Gold: the Peacock Room
1876-7, Freer Gallery of Art, Washington

Hanging on the far wall and acting as a key to the decorative ensemble, Whistler's painting *La Princesse du Pays de Porcelaine*

(1863-64) reigns over the sole surviving example of the artist's genius as an interior designer. During the creation of this interior he was described as "spending his days on ladders and scaffolding, lying on a hammock, painting with a brush fastened to a fishing-rod."

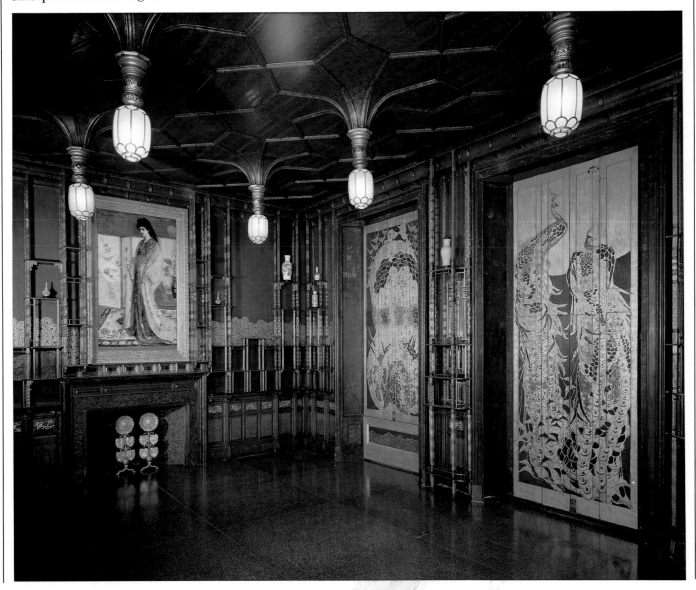

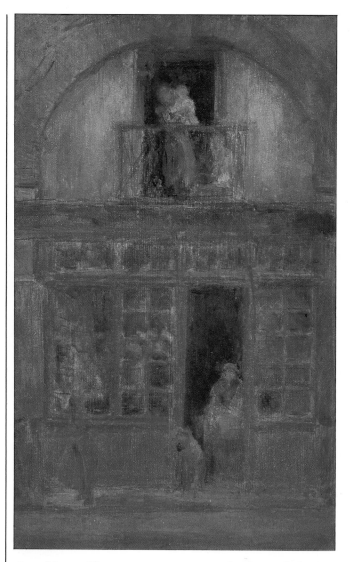

JAMES MCNEILL WHISTLER
A Shop with a Balcony
c1897-79, Hunterian Museum
and Art Gallery, University of
Glasgow

This delicate sketch, painted
in Dieppe, was executed on a
gray-primed panel the size of a
cigar box. It could almost be a
watercolor. Its mood of quiet
intimacy, its color and
geometry suggest the
paintings of the younger
generation of French avant-
garde artists of the period,
Bonnard and Vuillard, who
also found poetry in
unpretentious street scenes
such as this.

The aesthetic position

A year later he returned to England to pick up the pieces
of his shattered career. The process was a slow one, but
Victorian values were waning, the intellectual climate
was more favorably disposed to his ideas, and his
Venetian etchings were popular. In 1885 he publicized
his theories of aestheticism in the famous *10 o'clock
Lecture,* which he delivered to select audiences in
London, Oxford and Cambridge. This was a clear, witty
and occasionally poetic exposition of his creed. He pro-

tested vehemently against the accepted belief that
"Nature is always right" by putting forward the contrary
view that Nature is usually wrong, "that is to say, the condition of things that shall bring about the perfection of
harmony worthy of a picture is rare, and not common at
all … Nature contains all the elements, in color and
form, of all pictures, as the keyboard contains the notes
of all music. But the artist is born to pick, and choose, and
group with science, these elements, that the result may
be beautiful — as the musician gathers his notes, and
forms his chords, until he brings forth from chaos
beautiful harmony."

It is not surprising that an artist who took such care
with his paintings, frames and settings should take equal
care with the arrangement of his exhibitions. The rooms
in which his works were hung were invariably designed
with great simplicity and elegance. In 1881 the gallery in
which his Venetian pastels were shown was decorated
with a high-placed dark green dado which was separ-
ated from a narrow frieze of pink by a gilt moulding, the
gold being repeated in a deeper tone across the skirting
board. He designed a different decorative scheme for
each of his subsequent exhibitions and his concern for
achieving the best possible lighting of his works led to his
invention of a muslin hanging which filtered the direct
sunlight throughout the interior to create an acceptable
level of dispersed light.

By the 1890s Whistler's position as a master of the
evocative and the beautiful was established. In 1885
Stéphane Mallarmé translated his *10 o'clock Lecture* into
French, and appreciative pieces by other leading writers
began to appear in the French press. By the 1890s he had
become a cult figure for the young artists and writers of
the day; Oscar Wilde modeled his cult of the self on
Whistler and attempted — not always successfully — to
outwit and outdress the American dandy.

In 1892 a retrospective exhibition featuring forty-
three of his works was held at Goupil's London Gallery. It
was a public and critical success. Shortly after the exhibition, which had given him the satisfaction of reversing
the tables on the English art establishment, Whistler left
the country to settle once again in Paris, and in the same
year his *Portrait of the Artist's Mother* was bought by the
French state and entered the Luxembourg Museum.

In the summer of 1888 he married Beatrix (Trixie),
the widow of the architect, E. W. Godwin, ungallantly
abandoning Maud Franklin, his mistress of fifteen years
standing, and he and his new wife resumed the pattern
of restless traveling. In 1898 he was elected first
President of the International Society of Sculptors,

WHISTLER'S PAINTING METHODS

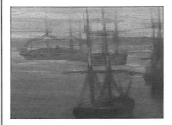

In *Valparaiso*, Whistler used very dilute pigment, thinned with a mixture of gasoline or turpentine.

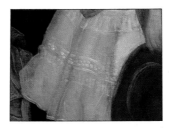

The transparent dress in the portrait of Miss Cicely Alexander was finalized only after continual rubbing down of previous attempts.

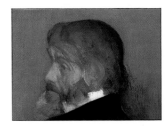

The head of Thomas Carlyle reveals nothing of the anguished hours of scraping down and reworking.

Whistler's technique was a quirky mixture of methods of painting learned at Gleyre's academy in the 1850s together with a series of improvisations directly onto the canvas. When working on large paintings, he used a three-foot long mahogany table as his "palette," arranging an array of mixed colors and tones on it with meticulous care, saying on one occasion, "If you cannot manage your palette how are you going to manage your canvas?" He worked with a fully loaded brush, holding it firmly and applying paint to canvas in a single confident sweep, standing at a distance from the canvas in order to balance the emerging forms with his subject. His long-handled brushes were specially made for him, and he also had a particular liking for large house-painter's brushes, his favorite being one to which he gave the name of Matthew. In place of the traditional mahlstick he preferred to use a walking cane.

Whistler always strove for a restrained and harmonious effect, avoiding excessive color and strong tonal contrasts, and unlike the Impressionists he never worked on a white canvas, always pre-tinting his ground a mid-gray, warm brown, red or sometimes even black. He would not begin a painting until he had prepared it, tone for tone, on his table-top "palette." In his portraits, the accents of tone would become sharper and sharper as the session progressed, and at the end of it the painting was either declared finished, or it was washed down with spirits in preparation for a fresh start the following session. His perfectionism was such that his unfortunate subjects often had to endure endless sittings.

For his *Portrait of Miss Cicely Alexander* (detail below), Whistler organized his table-top palette in the following way. In the center he placed a large mass of flake white. To the left of this were ranged light yellow to browns, and to the right were the reds, gradating to blues at the cool end of the color-temperature scale. Below the central white was a band of black, the extremities of which were used for mixing flesh and background hues.

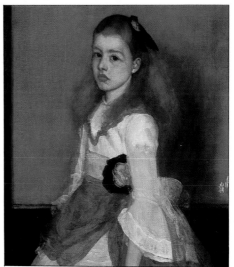

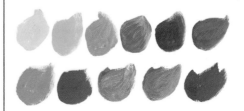

1 lemon yellow; 2 cadmium yellow; 3 yellow ocher; 4 raw sienna; 5 raw umber; 6 burnt sienna; 7 vermilion; 8 Venetian (or Indian) red; 9 rose madder; 10 cobalt blue; 11 Antwerp (mineral) blue

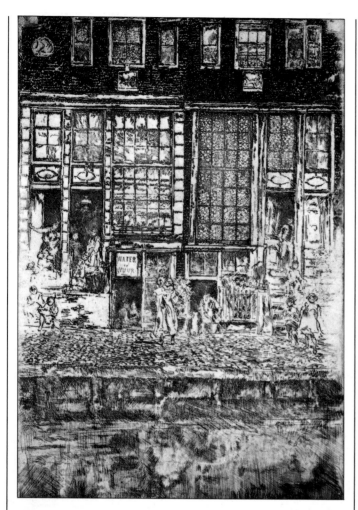

anecdote and print, and a sense of loneliness pervades most of his late works. The final decades of his life, during which he continued to travel, were dogged by ill health and a growing sense of isolation, despite the adulation accorded him by his acolytes to whom he was simply "the Master." He died on July 17, 1903 and was buried beside his wife in Chiswick cemetery not far from the tomb of Hogarth, whose works were the first that he is known to have admired.

JAMES MCNEILL WHISTLER
The Embroidered Curtain
1889, Freer Gallery of Art, Washington

Whistler is generally acknowledged to have been one of the finest printmakers of the modern period. His graphic work reveals a control over the technical aspects of the medium that is sometimes lacking in his oils. This etching not only shows his debt to Vermeer and 17th-century Dutch art, but also provides evidence of his love of children.

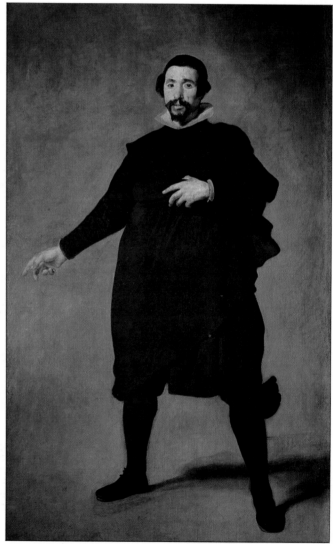

Painters and Gravers, a position which he held until his death.

Whistler's last years were weighed down with official honors from the continent, but it is sad to record that his paintings received no serious recognition from the official art institutions of the United Kingdom — with the notable exception of the Glasgow City Art Gallery.

Since the 1860s Whistler had always found it difficult to sustain a cordial relationship with anyone for long, and his friendships often resulted in quarrels and litigation. But before his wife died in 1896 after a prolonged illness, he made a number of touching drawings, lithographs and paintings of her that suggest a more sensitive side to his personality than that recorded in

DIEGO VELASQUEZ
Portrait of Pablo de Valladolid
c1632-33, Prado, Madrid

The unity of characterization and formal harmony made Velasquez' full-length portraits a model for generations of portraitists. A photograph of this painting was found in Whistler's studio at his death, and his own late self-portrait (right) was obviously based on it.

JAMES MCNEILL WHISTLER
Brown and Gold: a Self-portrait
c1896, Hunterian Museum and
Art Gallery, University of
Glasgow

This poignant self-portrait,
barely visible, is all that
remains of a more finished
work that Whistler rubbed
down in 1900. It is a powerful
image of the effect of time
upon an individual, and has
all the melancholy dignity of
the Velasquez portrait it is
based upon (left). It gives the
modern viewer a very
different picture of the artist
than the one handed down by
anecdote and contemporary
description.

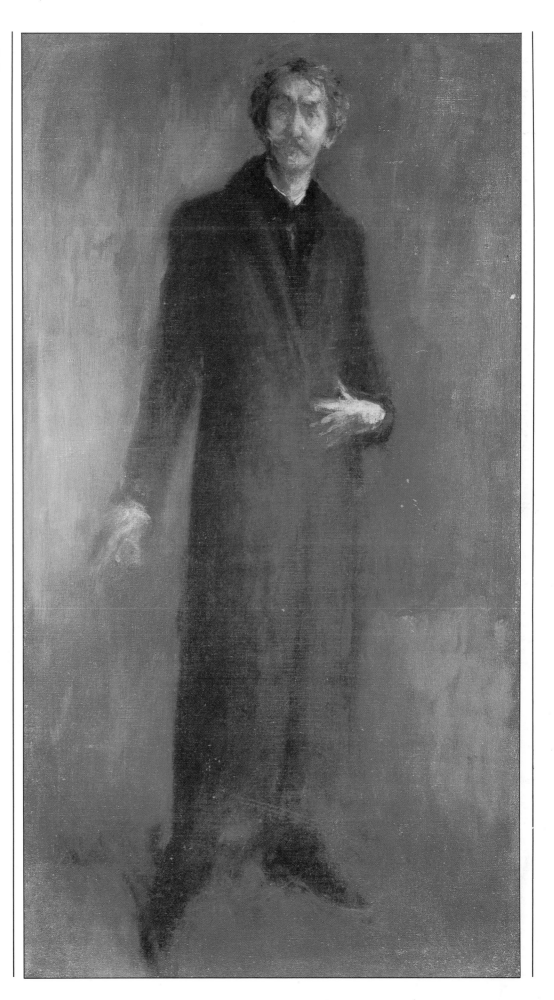

CHRONOLOGY OF WHISTLER'S LIFE

1834   July 11: James Abbott Whistler born in Lowell, Massachusetts.

1842   Major George Washington Whistler employed as engineer on Moscow-St Petersburg Railway; takes his family to Russia.

1851   Whistler enters West Point Academy, adds mother's maiden name, McNeill, to his own.

1854   Discharged from West Point for failing chemistry examination.

1855   November 2: Whistler arrives in Paris.

1856   Enters Charles Gleyre's studio, meets George du Maurier, Edward Poynter. Becomes close friend of Degas and Courbet.

1857   Visits Manchester Art Treasures Exhibition at Manchester, where he sees the work of Velasquez, the pre-Raphaelites and a selection of Japanese prints.

1858   *Twelve Etchings from Nature*, first major set of graphic work.

1860   *At the Piano* shown at Royal Academy.

1862   Settles in London.

1863   *The White Girl* shown at Salon des Refusés together with Edouard Manet's *Déjeuner sur l'herbe*.

1866   Travels to Valparaiso, Chile; paints first nocturnal scenes.

1871   Begins work on *Arrangement in Gray and Black: Portrait of the Artist's Mother* (bought by Musée du Luxembourg in 1891).

1876   Works on decorations for Francis Leyland's house at Prince's Gate, London, completed February, 1877; Leyland is displeased, only pays him half the '2000 guineas the artist claimed as his fee.

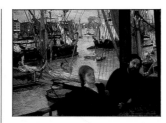

Wapping

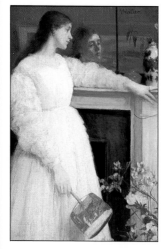

Symphony in White No.2: the Little White Girl

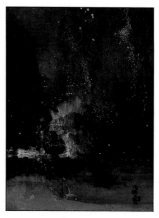

Nocturne in Black and Gold: the Falling Rocket

1877   Exhibits eight paintings at newly opened Grosvenor Gallery, including *Nocturne in Black and Gold: The Falling Rocket*, which is criticized by Ruskin. Whistler sues the critic for libel.

1878   November: Whistler awarded a farthing's damages without costs in his libel action against Ruskin; in severe financial difficulties.

1879   Leaves for Venice, stays for a year working on etchings and pastels of the city.

1881   Beginning of friendship with Oscar Wilde.

1885   February 20: First delivery of the *10 o'clock Lecture* at Prince's Hall, London.

1888   Through Claude Monet, meets Stéphane Mallarmé, the French Symbolist poet, who translates the *10 o'clock Lecture* into French. Marries Beatrice Godwin, widow of architect E. W. Godwin, designer of Whistler's former Chelsea home, the White House (1878-79).

1889   Major exhibition in New York; awarded first-class medal at Munich and Cross of St Michael of Bavaria.

1890   Publishes *The Gentle Art of Making Enemies*.

1892   Made Officer of Légion d'Honneur; major retrospective at Goupil Gallery in London.

1896   Wife dies, after long and painful illness.

1898   Teaching at Académie Carmen in Paris.

1903   July 17: Whistler dies in London.

1904   Memorial exhibition in Boston.

1905   Large memorial exhibition in London and Paris.

THE PAINTINGS

HARMONY IN GREEN AND ROSE: THE MUSIC ROOM

1860

Oil on canvas

37⅝×27⅞in/95.5×70.8cm

Freer Gallery of Art, Washington

The setting for this picture was the music room in the London home of Whistler's brother-in-law Seymour Haden. Haden was an influential printmaker of the period, specializing in drypoint and *plein-air* techniques (working outdoors, directly from the subject), and his influence on Whistler's work was considerable.

While it was being produced, the painting was referred to as *The Morning Call,* a title which links it to the work of some of the more conventional painters of the period, such as Alfred Stevens, who depicted the social round of the elegant upper middle-classes. The standing figure, Isabella Boott, a friend of the family, is dressed *"à l'Amazone"* as the fashionable ladies who rode their horses in the parks of London and Paris were called. Having fulfilled her social obligations, she is now making her farewells to her hostess, whose reflected image can be seen in the mirror. The young girl dressed in white, sitting absorbed in her book and taking little notice of the proceedings, is Annie Haden, Seymour's daughter.

The painting owes much to the Dutch art of the 17th century, and its interest in spatial depth suggests a close study of the work of Ingres. But like so much of Whistler's work, it has the quality of evoking a mood rather than presenting the viewer with an easily readable narrative, despite the number of figures and the rich detail. When the artist saw the painting again at his retrospective in 1892 he wrote to his wife that it looked, "quite primitive — but such *sunshine*! None of the Dutchmen to *compare* with it — and such color!"

Whistler painted this with the work of Parisian avant-garde artists very much in mind, and his innovatory treatment of space parallels the work of artists such as Degas and Manet. Degas noted the similarity of their artistic ambitions at this time. "In our beginnings," he said, "Fantin [Fantin-Latour], Whistler and I were on the same road, the road from Holland." Dutch landscapes and *genre* scenes offered a serious alternative to the vast historical or mythological canvases, known as *machines,* that were favored by the artistic establishment of the day. They were an inspiration to the new wave of artists who were beginning to reject academic subject matter in favor of depicting scenes of everyday life. This ambitious painting was clearly conceived in these terms, and represents a major achievement for an artist who was then only twenty-six years old.

Whistler repainted the head of Annie, and it seems that the mirror-reflection of the hostess, Deborah Haden, Whistler's sister and Seymour's wife, was a later addition. Certainly her presence makes the painting easier to interpret. The work is painted on a very coarse canvas, although its texture is only apparent in the thinly painted area of the skirt. Nearly a third of the canvas surface is taken up by the cream, green and deep pink of the chintz drapery, and this emphasizes the flat decorative quality of the work and contrasts with the powerfully realized deep space of the picture. The daring divisions of space and the continuance of the picture's action beyond the confines of the canvas anticipate Whistler's later use of Japanese compositional motifs and Degas' later and possibly more familiar works.

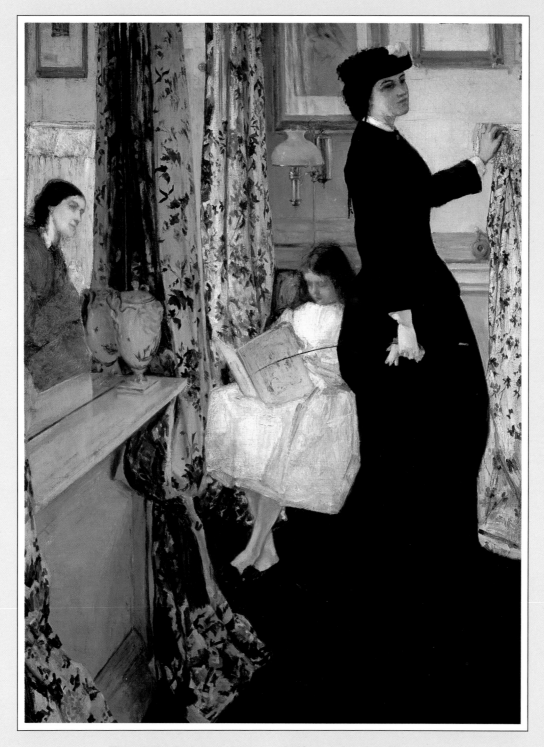

The painting is characterized by a Vermeer-like organization of pictorial space. The clearly defined silhouettes and strong light source are stylistic features typical of the work of the Dutch master. A sharp diagonal leads the eye to the hidden window through which the clear morning light streams, casting white highlights upon the brilliantly patterned chintz which animates what would otherwise be a rather monochromatic picture.

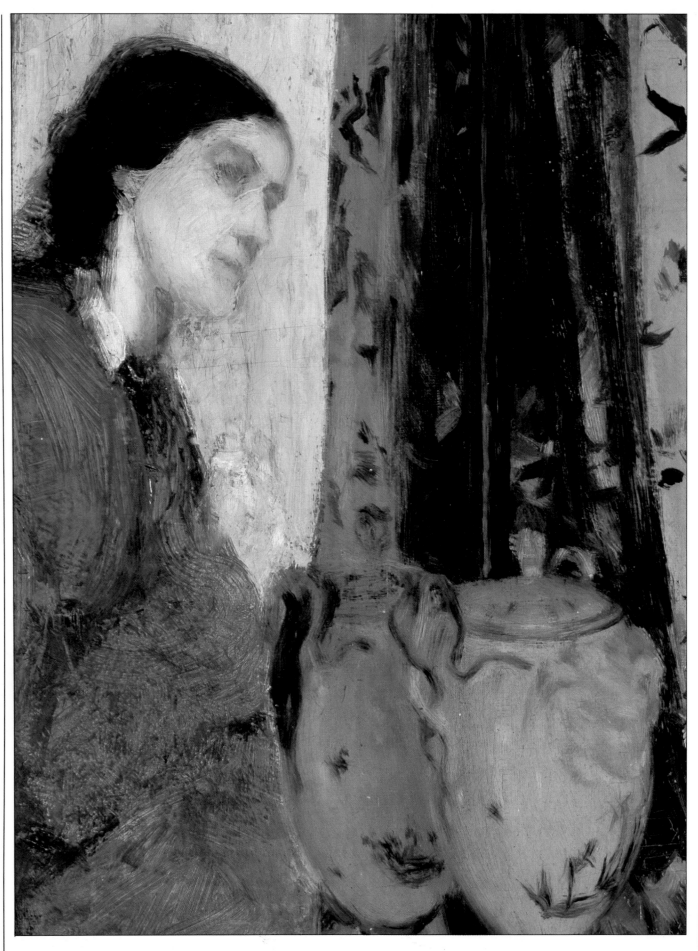

1 *Actual size detail*

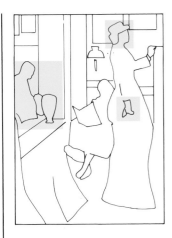

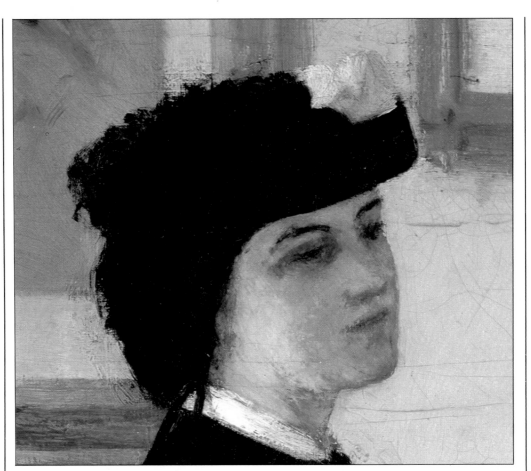

2

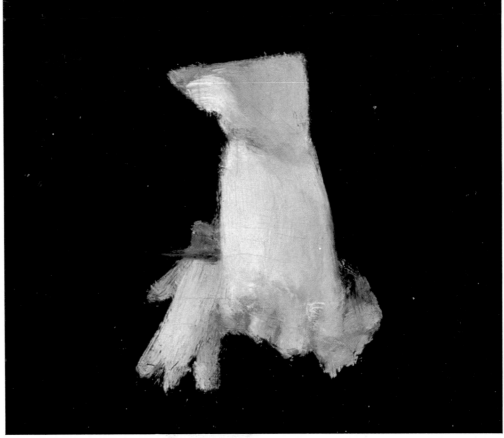

3

1 *Actual size detail* The head of Deborah, Whistler's sister, is seen reflected in the mirror, a motif that fascinated the artist. The figure, worked in thin glazes of loosely brushed paint, is seen against an area of light and opaque paint which highlights the reflective nature of the mirror surface and gives a tonal balance to the painting. By reversing the color balance of the chintz, Whistler has used greens to suggest shade. The fluency with which the snake-handled pot is drawn is unusual in his work, and suggests the suave handling of his American admirer William Sargent, whose portraits owe much to Whistler's example.

2 The figure of Isabella Boott, a friend of Whistler's brother-in-law, has a sharpness of focus that contrasts with the soft modelling of her features and the scumbled paint that describes the edge of her hat. Her body is crisply delineated and reduced to the simplest of tonal contrasts. In comparison with the work of the Impressionists, working a decade later, the form is relatively unaffected by the fall of light.

3 The starkness of the contrast between the gloved hand and the black dress acts as a perfect foil to the subtle modulations of tone and spatial ambiguities of the rest of the painting.

WAPPING

Signed and dated 1861 (not completed until 1864)
Oil on canvas
28×40in/71.1×101.6cm
National Gallery of Art, Washington

This ambitious canvas was painted shortly after Whistler had decided to make London his home, and like his other paintings and etchings of the river Thames it reveals his deep love of the busy waterway. The painting is based upon the solid principles of the French Realist tradition to which Whistler had been introduced by the work of Courbet. But on this framework, he has imposed a compositional design that possibly owes its genesis to his awareness of Japanese prints. He had first come across these at the Manchester Art Treasures Exhibition of 1857, and by the 1860s he was collecting them, together with the blue and white Nanking porcelain he admired so much. The asymmetrical structure of the balcony, the relative size of the figures to the background and the clarity of the composition as a whole are familiar devices in Oriental art. The work may also owe something to both the new art of photography and Whistler's knowledge of the work of etcher Charles Meryon and his painter and printmaker friend Alphonse Legros; he described the background as being, "like an etching."

Given the complexities of the project, it is hardly surprising that it took so long to complete and underwent many revisions. Sadly, its condition has deteriorated over the years; as early as 1890 cracks "half an inch wide" were noticed on its surface. These were probably caused by Whistler ignoring one of the basic rules of oil painting: working fat over lean. To prevent cracking, a painting should be laid in with a dilute pigment, while later layers can be thicker, with more oil in the pigment. If there is too much oil in the lower layer it will dry too slowly and contract when it hardens, setting up a tension which causes cracks in the upper layers. Whistler's later changes in technique restricted this problem to his early works.

Wapping reveals Whistler's remarkable ability to simplify and codify the complexity of the scene before him, although the final image was not achieved without a struggle. The shipping is rendered with an almost dry brush dragged over a relatively thinly painted background. All the incidental details of the rigging and masts are accurately described. Whistler's preference for tone as opposed to luminosity or color is shown by the predominance of beiges, browns, whites and grays throughout the painting.

The picture was begun at an inn called the Angel on the Rotherhithe side of the Thames, and Whistler worked at his "masterpiece," as he termed it, in great secrecy, making constant changes as the work progressed. According to his own description of it, the painting was very different in mood and coloration to what we see today. "I've succeeded in getting an expression! ... a real expression. Ah! Let me tell you about the head: there is a quantity of hair, the most beautiful you've ever seen! a red hot gilded, but coppered — like everything Venetian you've dreamed about! ... And with this first-rate expression I'm talking about, an air of saying to her sailor: 'All that's very fine, my fellow, but I've seen others of your sort!' You know, she winks, and she makes fun of him. Now all this against the light and consequently in a half-tint/tone that is atrociously difficult ... Ssh! not a word to Courbet!" The figure of Whistler's model and mistress Jo Hiffernan, as the waterside prostitute, was presumably a little more risqué originally, and the rather more subdued characterization that finally appeared on the canvas can be seen as a response to the work of the pre-Raphaelites. In 1863 the artist introduced the white-shirted figure of his friend Legros, which considerably adds to the enigmatic nature of the painting, but its essentially realistic nature makes it an interesting foil to the more decorative views of the river that he produced throughout his later career (see page 43).

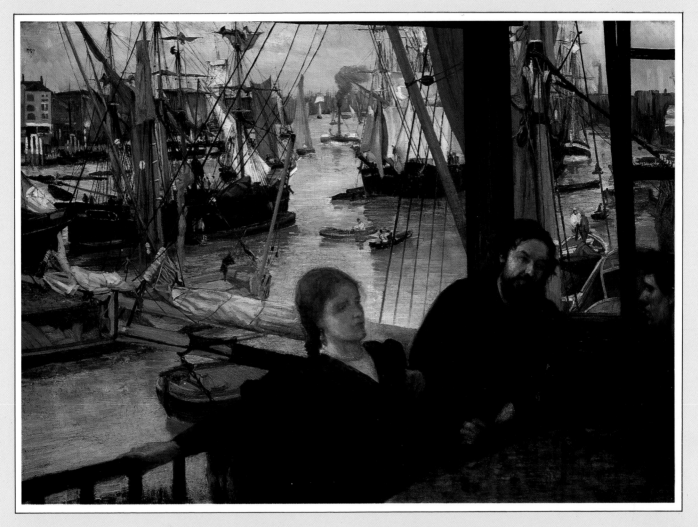

The art critic of *The Times* wrote of one of Whistler's pictures of the Thames that "If Velasquez had painted our river he would have painted it something in this style." The artist was deeply influenced by Velasquez throughout his career, and his avoidance of an overt narrative and refusal to exploit the potentially sentimental qualities of the subject — a beautiful woman, a sailor and another man — must certainly have owed much to the cool and ordered art of the Spanish master.

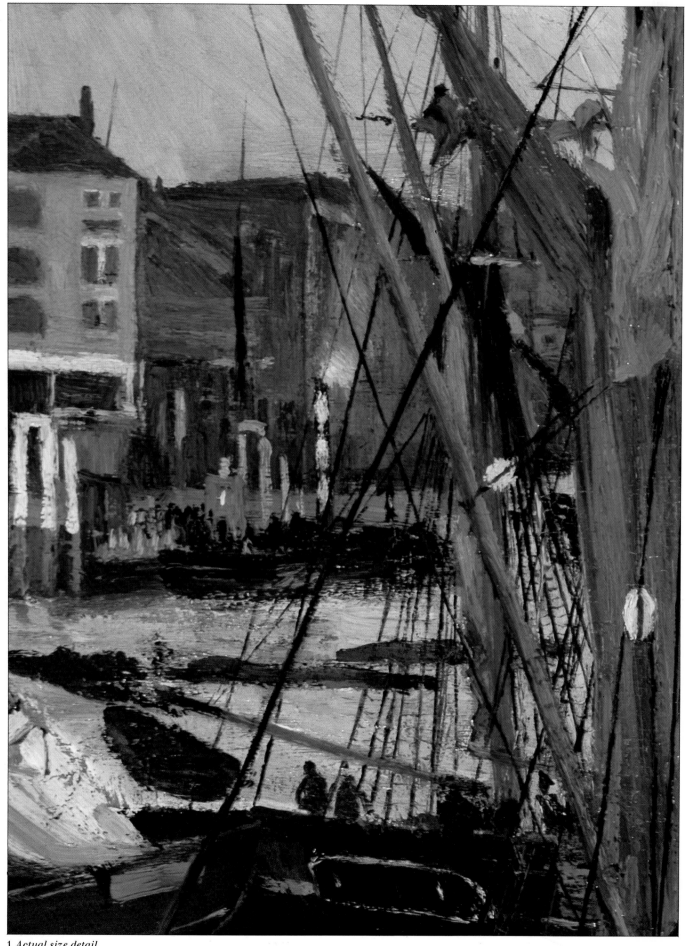

1 *Actual size detail*

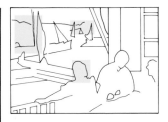

1 *Actual size detail* The river beyond the balcony is a mass of activity, each incident expressed with the most economical of means. The rapid brushstrokes and blocky slabs of paint look forward to the early works of Monet, who was equally captivated by such scenes. Except for a few sharp accents of pure color, the overall harmony of the painting is set by the warm ochers and velvety blacks of the buildings and boats shown in this detail.

2 The positioning of the red smoke stack directly above the head of the girl suggests a triangular form, and brings a sense of order to the composition. This detail shows the surprisingly varied range of Whistler's brushwork, from the impasto of the water breaking against the bow of the boat to the sharp splinters of paint that suggest the masts of distant vessels set against the thinly applied lilac tones of the warehouses.

3 Despite the realistic qualities of this painting, Whistler has made adjustments to the scene as it would have been perceived in actuality. The woman is placed against the light (an effect known as *contre-jour*), and would appear to the viewer to be in silhouette. However, Whistler has lightened the tones of the head but lowered the focus, which has the effect of taking the eye through to the imagined space behind.

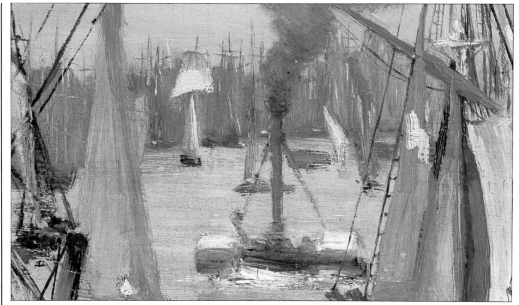

2

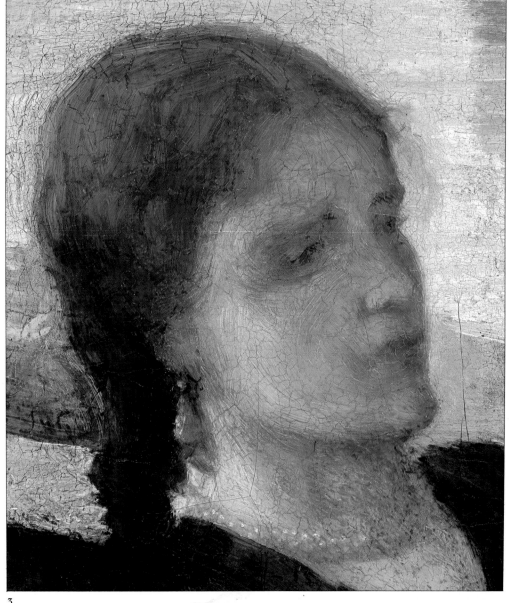

3

SYMPHONY IN WHITE NO. 2:
THE LITTLE WHITE GIRL

1864

Oil on canvas

30×20in/76×51cm

Tate Gallery, London

This is one of the most exquisite of all Whistler's paintings. His mistress Jo Hiffernan is seen in a mood of wistful reverie, gazing into a mirror which reflects in subdued tones the gentle melancholy of her face. This quiet interpretation is very much Whistler's own creation, and suggests little of the fiery nature of the Irish girl who was his constant companion, favored model and occasional business manager. In 1863 Whistler's mother came to London from America to live with her son, and Jo had to move out of the household, but when, a little later, his mother made a trip to Torquay to recover her health, Jo moved back to her former position. When Whistler went to Valparaiso in 1866 (see page 30) he made a will in which he ignored the rights of his mother, leaving all his possessions to Jo. Soon after his return to London the lovers parted on amicable terms, and Whistler's mother returned to her former place in her son's affections.

The Little White Girl marks a very definite move away from the art of Courbet who, in a letter of 1865 described Whistler as an "Englishman who is my pupil." Two years later the so-called "Englishman" wrote to Fantin-Latour revealing a somewhat different view of their relationship. "Courbet and his influence was disgusting... I am not complaining of the influence his painting had on my own. He did not have any, and it can't be found in my canvases. It is because that damned Realism made an immense appeal to my painter's vanity, and, disregarding all traditions, cried aloud to me the assurance of ignorance: 'Long live Nature! Nature, my dear fellow, that cry was a great misfortune to me."

The formal qualities of the picture are masterly, the simplicity of the girl's white dress is the dominant feature of the canvas, while the Japanese fan and the chrysanthe-mums counterpoint the weight of the picture's interest, which is placed in the upper portion of the composition. Jo's head, her reflection and the oriental pots fill this upper register in a fascinating amalgam of differing textures, colors and forms. The model's neck and arm sweep down to the lower area of the painting, taking the viewer's eye back to the sketched-in details of the fan loosely held in the girl's right hand. Both this painting and the *White Girl* of 1862, which had been rejected by the French Salon, could be grouped, in pose and mood, with the work of such artists as Millais and Rossetti, who also had a fondness for images of women lost in tranquil reverie. Both artists had become good friends of Whistler, and encouraged him in his belief that the fundamental purpose of art was the creation of beauty.

The picture was exhibited at the Royal Academy show of that year. Attached to the frame was a poem by Algernon Swinburne entitled *Before a Mirror*, a shortened version of which appeared in his *Poems and Ballads* of 1866. In 1902 Whistler remarked that it was "a rare and graceful tribute from the poet to the painter — a noble recognition of a work by the production of a nobler one."

It was retouched at least once in 1900, when the artist removed the date which followed his signature, and either at this time or earlier he reduced the number of chrysanthe-mums and made other alterations, which can be seen on the canvas. The fireplace — which although it serves the composition well enough, is imperfectly drawn — was thought by Whistler's biographers, the Pennells, to have been the one in his own house in Lindsey Row. The mirror reflection may owe something to Ingres' use of similar motifs, but in handling suggests more the influence of Velasquez' famous *Rokeby Venus*.

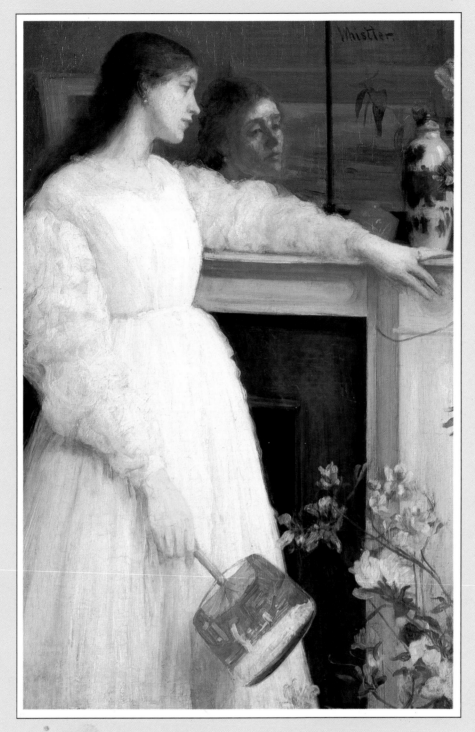

The painting's musical title suggests that this image of a pretty young girl should be regarded as a piece of "visual music" to delight the eyes. The picture's structure is founded on the simple T-shape formed by the model's dress. The whole picture is essentially an arrangement of cool grays, soft ochers and subtly modulated passages of white set off by sharp accents of red and blue.

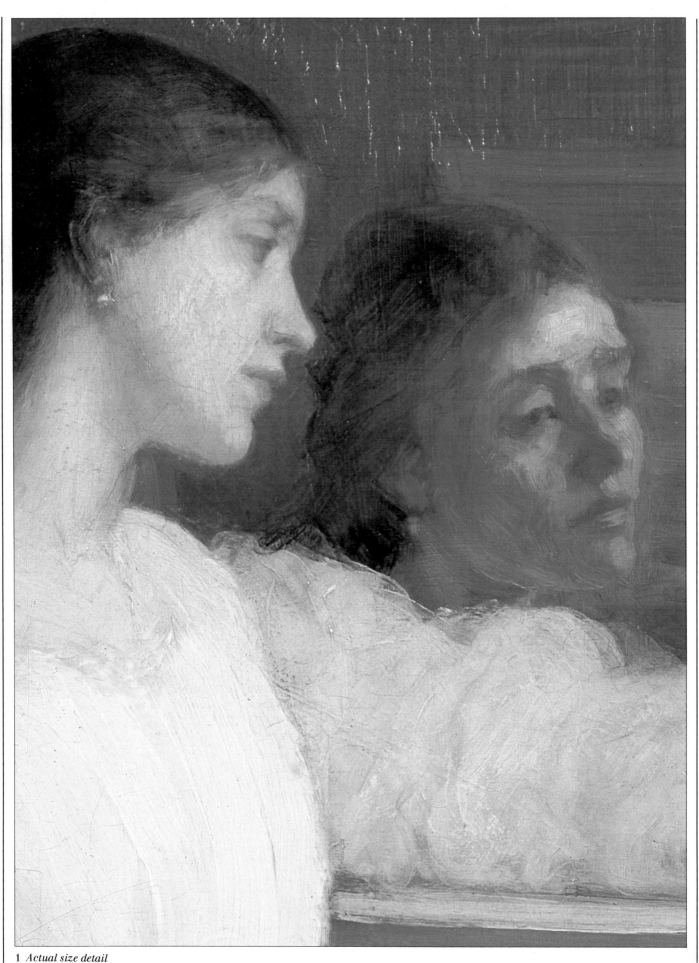

1 *Actual size detail*

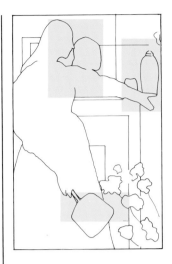

1 *Actual size detail* Like a piece of music, a work of art is as significant for what it suggests as for what it describes. Whistler's model Jo looks not at her own reflection but into the depths of the mirror itself, oblivious of the gaze of the viewer. In this detail the role of the mirror can be clearly appreciated: it provides a device which has allowed the artist to unite several disparate painting methods in the same image. The smooth handling of the girl's face contrasts with the bolder, more direct treatment of the reflection. As in Velasquez' famous *Rokeby Venus*, the reflected face is relatively crudely modeled, with directional brushwork and a few simple tones.

2,3 Contrasting with the smooth ochers and greys of the mirror area, the brilliant color of the small red pot and its reflection, together with the blue and white of the porcelain jar, echo the colours of the Japanese fan (3). The pot is painted wet-in-wet, the colors dragging into each other so that the brushwork suggests the smooth rounded form. A single vertical stroke of pure white made with a square brush describes the highlight and sets off the blue-white modulations of the pot, its design a forerunner of the butterfly that Whistler later adopted as his personal cypher. Against the pot, and picking up some of its color, is a delicate chrysanthemum bloom.

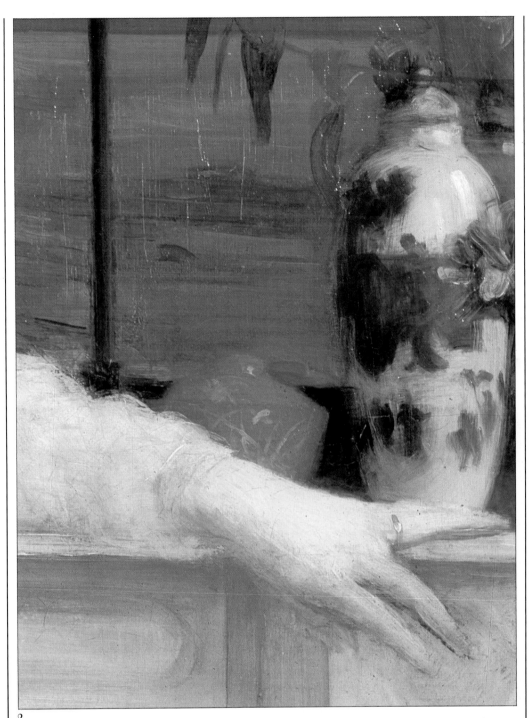

2

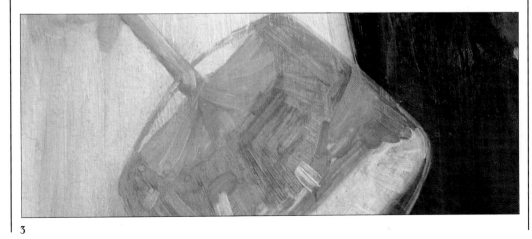

3

CREPUSCULE IN FLESH COLOR AND GREEN: VALPARAISO

1866
Oil on canvas
23×29¾in/58.4×75.5cm
Tate Gallery, London

In 1866, Whistler made a mysterious sea voyage to Valparaiso, in Chile, just at the time (March 31) when the Spanish fleet was bombarding the port in retaliation for Chile's support of Peru in a dispute with Spain. Why he should have made this journey at such a critical juncture in his career has never been explained. Perhaps he felt guilty, as a West Point man — albeit a failed one — of having missed the American Civil War, in which his younger brother, Charles, had served as a soldier and surgeon. Or perhaps he was simply seeking a diversion from his own artistic and personal problems. Whatever the reason, he boarded ship at Southampton, arrived at Valparaiso, and returned home after a few days spent in the ship, at anchor in the harbor.

The fruits of this odd escapade were a number of seascapes, of which this painting is one. Whistler told a friend that it was completed "at a single sitting, having prepared his colors in advance of the chosen hour," and an examination of the picture surface corroborates his statement. He has used a dark brown ground to unify the tones of the composition, while the sky has been swept in with what he referred to as his "sauce," a thinned-down paint which merges imperceptibly into the thicker paint of the sea. The basis of the "sauce" was a mixture of either gasoline or turpentine, with which he diluted his pigment so heavily that it was necessary to paint on highly absorbent canvases. Although this allowed him to create wonderfully subtle effects of tone, because the paint seeped into and fused with the weave of the canvas, it was a lethal mixture, and extremely detrimental to the picture's stability. Its advantage, from the immediate pictorial point of view, was that it gave him the means to create the impression of the painting being one continuous veil of modulated color, with the forms emerging mistily from an all-enveloping atmosphere. The entire painting is brushed from side to side with a number of long horizontal strokes which suggest the slow, heavy movement of the sea and the — beautifully observed — strands of delicately colored cloud formations. The paint surface is so thin that Whistler's preparatory drawing can be clearly seen underneath the boats, which were painted after he had established the sky and sea. The pencil lines are rapidly scribbled onto the canvas in a series of grouped striations which bear no descriptive relationship to maritime structures but simply record the verticality of the masts. To complete the image, a few touches of color are set down with great exactitude and feeling to bring the whole scene in focus.

The paintings of the French Impressionists, with their bright, prismatic color and broken brushwork, may seem very distant from this picture of Whistler's, but the painting that gave the Impressionist movement its name, Claude Monet's *Impression, Sunrise* of 1872, is much closer to Whistler's work than to that of his French counterparts. Monet knew Whistler, and admired his work, having probably seen some of the latter's early paintings by 1870, when he visited London.

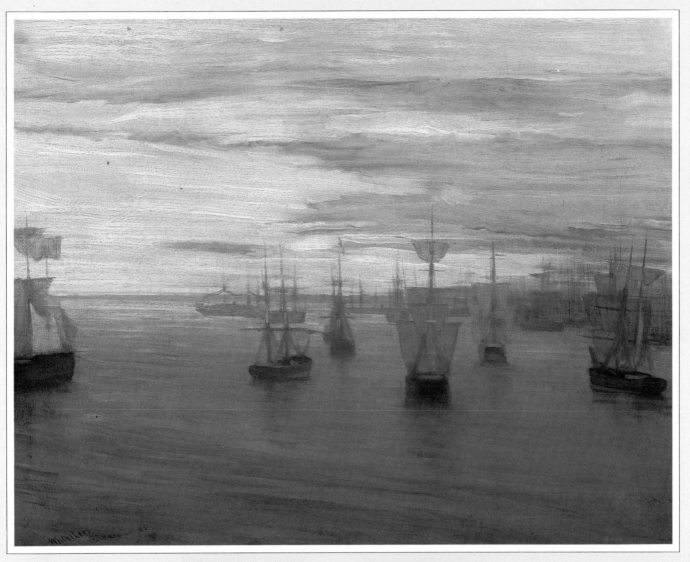

This convincing evocation of the beauty and stillness of the sea has been achieved with an apparent ease and the absolute minimum of means. All unnecessary detail has been suppressed: the complexity of the ships' rigging so evident in *Wapping* (see page 23) has here been reduced to a few simply drawn triangles of paint. The sheets of sail hang still in the mysterious glimmering light of the dusk, and the sun's recent departure is evident in the rich creamy white of the underlit clouds. We can sense the idle movement of the anchored vessels, as they rock gently with the tides and currents.

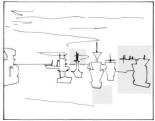

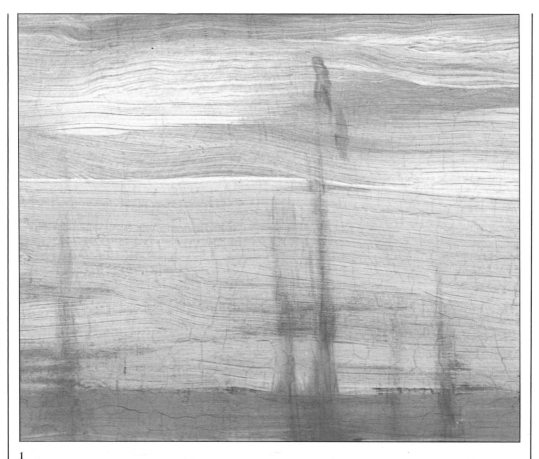

1

1 The effect of afterglow in the sky has been obtained in part by Whistler's habitual practice of painting on a dark ground. The centrally placed muted blue and red of the tricolor are the only pure colors in the composition. The absent white of the flag is suggested by the paint that describes the sky.

2 The coloristic beauty of this painting is matched by the sensitivity of the handling. The brushstrokes move, ever-responsive, across the canvas surface with the kind of delicacy and pace that one associates with Watteau. The brush has been allowed to twist and turn upon itself as it describes the movement of the clouds and water. The pressure with which the paint has been applied varies from area to area, in places causing delicate ridges to stand proud from the canvas surface.

3 *Actual size detail* The effect of the mass of shipping gathered close to shore on the right-hand side of the canvas has been gained by leaving the initial rapid pencil jottings half visible on the finished canvas. Presumably these marks were made at the outset of the painting, as they have been drawn with remarkable freedom, and stretch far into the sky area.

2

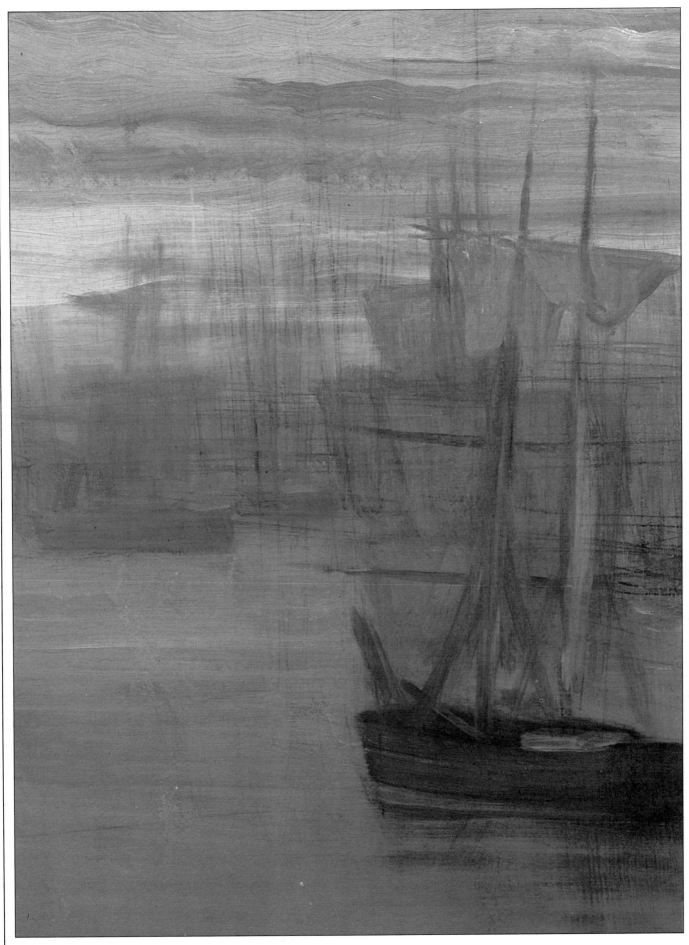

3 Actual size detail

Variations in Flesh Color and Green: the Balcony

1864-7
24¼×19⅜in/61.6×49cm
Oil on wood
Freer Gallery of Art, Washington

This painting is an example of one of Whistler's many attempts to paint his way out of the difficulties he found himself in during the 1860s. Its intention is clear enough: he hoped to produce an art of timeless beauty, motivated by his response to reality, but carefully ordering that reality by means of Japanese costumes and the conventions of Greek art. The results were not always successful, and by the end of the decade, he had abandoned this rather contrived approach and returned to the more natural theme of the river and its environs.

In this painting, the inclusion of a woman playing the Japanese three-stringed instrument called the *samisen* is a clear visual reference to music, as is the piano in his first major canvas, *At the Piano*, of 1859. Whistler wanted his paintings to be appreciated in an abstract way as pieces of visual music rather than for any narrative or descriptive qualities, and in 1867 he began to give them musical or abstract titles such as "nocturne" or "arrangement" (later retitling the early works). The relationship between music and art was the subject of great debate among avant-garde writers and painters throughout the 19th century. In 1834 the poet and novelist Théophile Gautier had published a short novel, *Mademoiselle du Maupin*, and in the preface of this influential and deliberately paradoxical book occur the following lines. "Things are beautiful in inverse proportion to their utility. The only thing that is truly beautiful is a thing that serves no purpose at all." Beauty, it was believed, should stand proud and aloof from the world, its deadliest enemies being the twin evils of utility and progress. Whistler himself reacted strongly against the Victorian idea that the artist's purpose was to provide a blueprint for public morality, believing that a work of art should exist in its own right, independent of prosaic reality.

By utilizing aspects of Oriental art in his work, he was able to create images that contained attractively mysterious and exotic qualities corresponding to his Western audiences' preconceptions of the East. The Japanese borrowings are obvious, and have been identified by a number of authorities. Four women, dressed in Oriental robes, are shown in a setting that relates directly to the work of the printmaker Harunobu, who like other artists of the Ukiyo-e school, depicted life in the brothels of Edo. The European features of Whistler's women and the view over the Thames to Battersea, however, situates the painting firmly in the West.

Like many 19th-century artists, Whistler has here presented the women as no more than passive decorative objects. In this respect the painting's true antecedents are Ingres' odalisques and Delacroix's *Women of Algiers*. The quirky mixture of stylistic elements is only just held in check. The railings are shown parallel to the picture surface, balanced by the two half-furled blinds. The expanse of the balcony floor suggests the artist's high viewpoint, recalling the directness of his *Wapping* painting (see page 23), and also vividly suggesting the presence of the artist — and hence the viewer. The standing figure looking out over the river links the foreground with the tonally correct backdrop of the far side of the river, complete with its warehouses and chimneys. The tension contained between these two very different worlds is complemented both by Whistler's realistic treatment of the wharfside architecture on the far bank of the river and the strong surface pattern of the foreground. This tension is further amplified by the "realistic" butterflies crossing the rectangular enclosure that contains Whistler's distinctive mark, which appears in this painting for the first time. Whistler signed his work with a butterfly motif developed from his own monogram, and the same visual pun appears in *Miss Cicely Alexander* (see page 47).

34

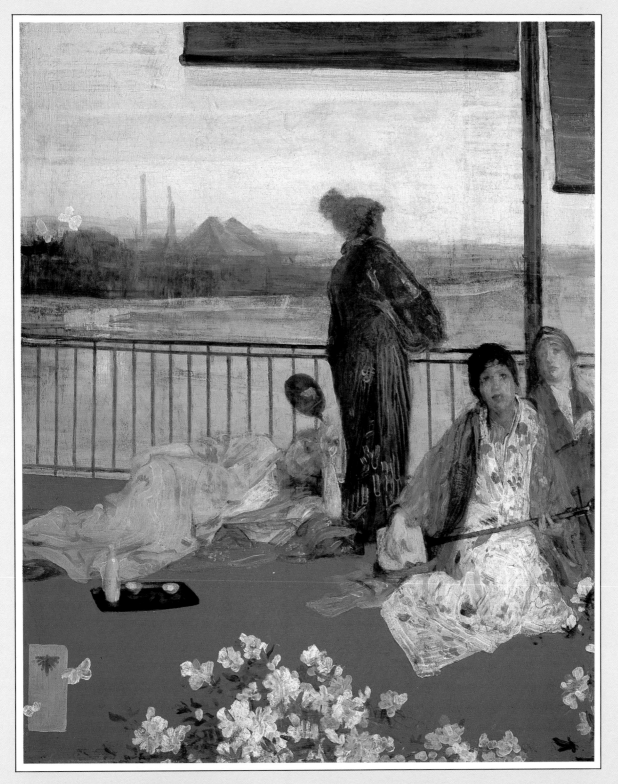

This is one of Whistler's Japanese "fancy dress" pictures, an intriguing medley of semi-erotic fantasy with the everyday setting of the bank of the Thames at Battersea. The contrived nature of the subject matter is matched by a wide range of stylistic mannerisms and visual puns, but these painterly devices do not destroy the melancholy and evocative mood of the painting, somewhat reminiscent of Degas' history and theater paintings of the early 1860s.

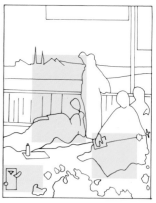

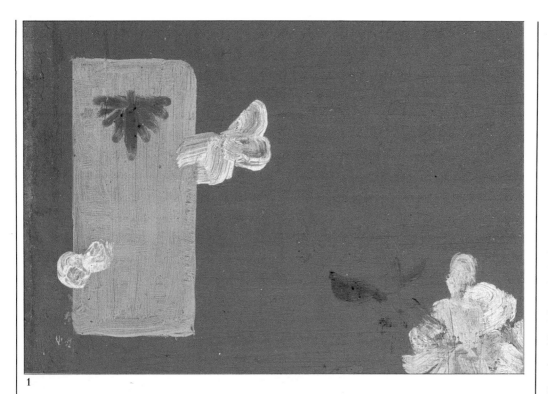

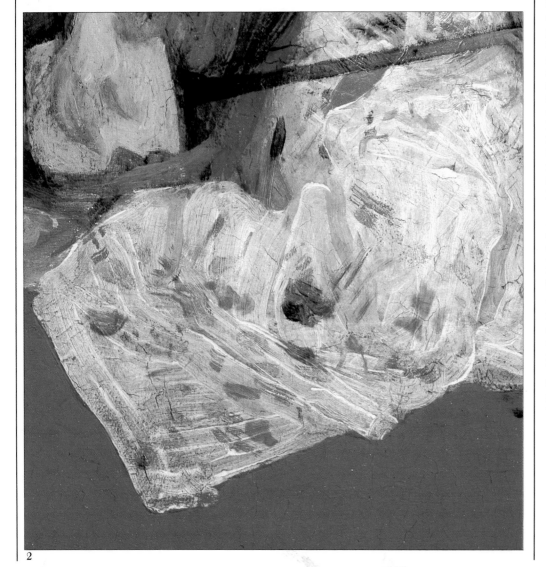

1 Whistler has here repeated the colors of the reclining figure of the cartouche which contains his butterfly insignia. Against this are seen two of a group of butterflies which, in their turn, are made up of the same brushmarks seen in the blossom which fills the lower area of the composition.

2 Whistler has again used the lilac blue and warm, deep red of his *Wapping* painting (see page 23). His lack of concern for anatomical exactitude relates to the stylizations seen in Japanese prints, and the same influence is discernible in the crisply drawn folds and edges of the kimono. The lightly painted garment reveals the gray of the floor beneath, and the delicately rendered pattern picks up color found elsewhere in the picture.

3 *Actual size detail* The surface of the panel shows the effect of the artist's habitual practice of scraping down previously worked areas before repainting. The grain of the panel can be clearly seen in places, and part of the river area has been painted on top of the uniform mid-gray of the floor. The reclining figure has been loosely brushed on top of the railings painted earlier, and traces of them are still visible beneath the kimono.

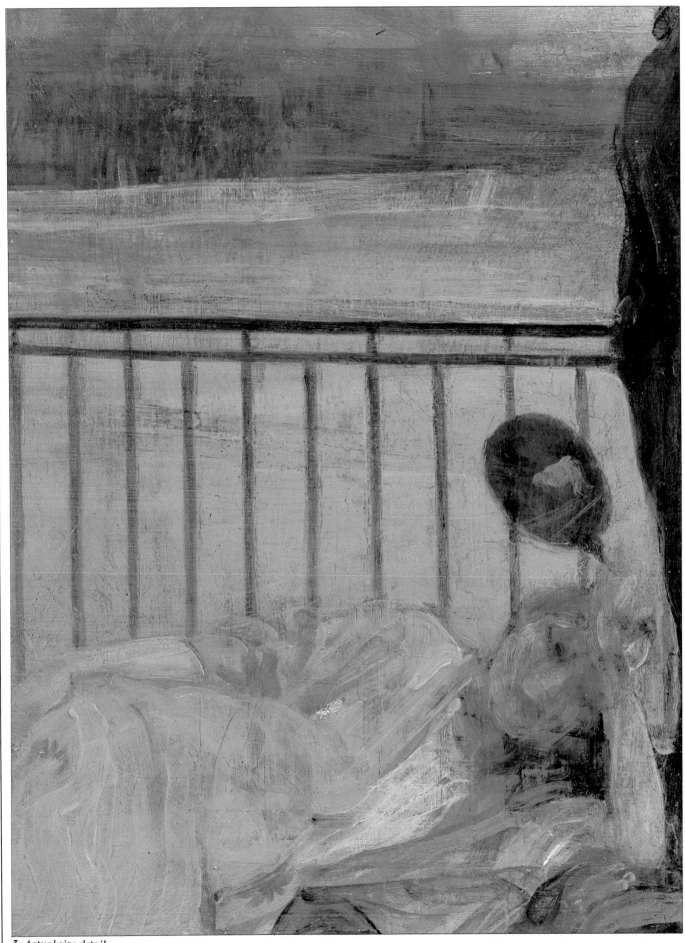

3 *Actual size detail*

HARMONY IN FLESH COLOR AND RED

(formerly *Symphony in Red*)
c 1869
$15\frac{1}{4} \times 14$in/38.7×35.6cm
Oil on canvas
Museum of Fine Arts, Boston

During the mid-1860s Whistler became obsessed with the idea of producing a series of paintings that would combine the grace and simplicity of the Greek terracotta statuettes known as Tanagra figures with the stylish exoticism of Japanese design as he knew it from Oriental prints and artefacts. The woodcuts of the Japanese artist Kiyonaga seemed to have served as the fundamental model for his designs; but as his entire collection of prints was sold after his bankruptcy in 1879, it is impossible to say what his collection consisted of at this time.

Whistler's work of this period contains strong elements of the French Neo-Grecian school of painting, of which his first master, Charles Gleyre, was one of the best-known practitioners, but it was seeing the work of Albert Moore in 1865 that spurred him on to attempt an art of a similar abstract power. Moore's paintings invariably depicted groups of young "flower-like women," as Swinburne referred to them. They were placed either in an enclosed setting or on a seashore, engaged in doing nothing in particular, their dress and manner deliberately non-specific, but suggesting at once an Oriental, Classical and modern character. The fashions of the women in *Harmony in Flesh Color and Red,* despite their generalized nature, are actually those current in the late 1860s. The painting was produced about 1869 and relates to the series of decorative paintings that he called the *Six Projects,* which are now in the Freer Gallery of Art, Washington, but were originally intended for Sir Francis Leyland. Unfortunately Whistler was unable to bring his designs to completion. The one that was finished he felt unhappy about, and he tried repeatedly but unsuccessfully to buy it back from its owner.

The title of this painting is not Whistler's own, but no doubt he would have approved of its musical associations. It shows three women dressed in a vivid red conversing in an interior or on a terrace; their manner is relaxed and casual, they could almost be models in the studio of a Royal Academy member, waiting to pose for one of those sentimental canvases so popular with the 19th-century public, and which Whistler professed to despise so much. In fact the painting could relate to his own unsuccessful attempts to produce a large version of Courbet's *The Painter in his Studio.* Certainly the figures have the air of quiet expectancy that we find in Degas' images of ballet dancers waiting to go on stage or the models of Seurat's painting of his studio, known as the *Poseuses.* The figure reaching down with an extraordinarily long arm to fit her shoe is an especially happy invention.

The lightness and delicacy of the technique could not be more distant from the earthy Realism of Courbet, an influence that had colored the artist's earlier paintings. It was at this time that Whistler was writing to his friend Fantin-Latour deploring the influence of Courbet and expressing his wish to overcome some of his shortcomings in the technical aspects of his art. He had expressed the regret that he had not trained with the artist Ingres, a consummate draughtsman, whom Degas admired above all others. But although some of Whistler's work does suffer from a lack of incisiveness in the drawing, in this example the fluidity of the brushwork used to block in the elegant forms of the women is perfectly matched to its role as a conveyor of the work's formal delights.

The butterfly monogram was a later addition to the painting, and it has been suggested that it was painted on by another hand, as the form it takes here relates to the work of the mid-1880s.

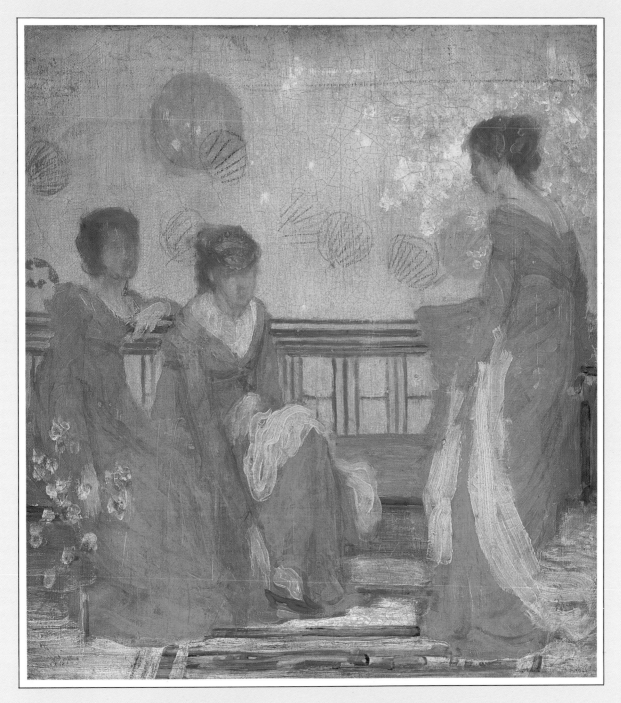

Like musical notations, rhythms of color, line and form move across this small canvas in harmonious counterpoint. No dominating central motif or detailed characterization disturb the picture's visual flow, and the viewer's eye moves across and around it. Regular intervals are provided by the uprights of the bench, balanced by the rise and fall of the models' heads and the scallop-like decorations on the wall that move in melodic progression across the picture surface.

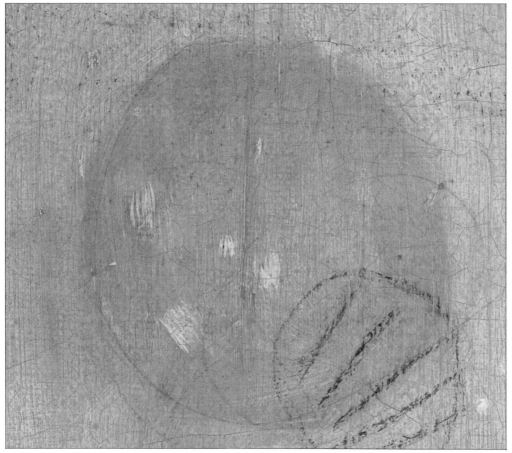

1

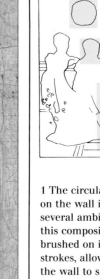

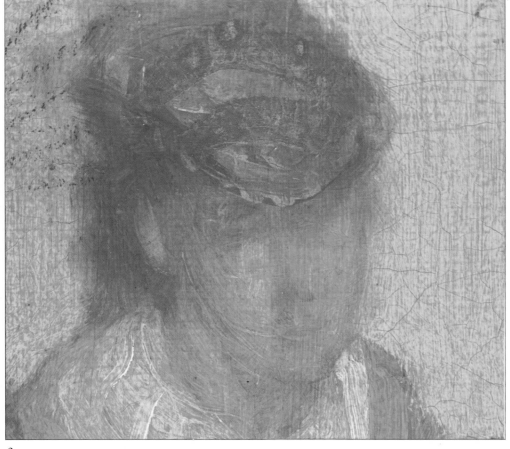

2

1 The circular orange design on the wall is only one of the several ambiguous elements in this composition. Its color is brushed on in thin vertical strokes, allowing the peach of the wall to show through in places. Touches of yellow and pink enrich the coloration and refer to the color harmonies in the picture as a whole. The pencil-drawn fan or scallop shapes that flit like butterfly wings across the wall create further textural interest.

2 The painting has a richness of color and texture that we associate with late Degas, while the musicality of design is comparable to Matisse's decorative works such as *La Danse* of 1909. The facial characteristics of the models are left undefined, in order not to disturb the aesthetic balance of the composition. Two simple areas of red pick up the barely discernible red of the lips and act as a visual link across the empty central portion of the composition.

3 A square brush leaves an easily recognizable trace in a series of staccato movements which complement the much more fluid painting of the drapery resting on the central figure's lap. Peaches, oranges, reds and browns are made to harmonize with a shrill mauve color that is softened with white on the bench.

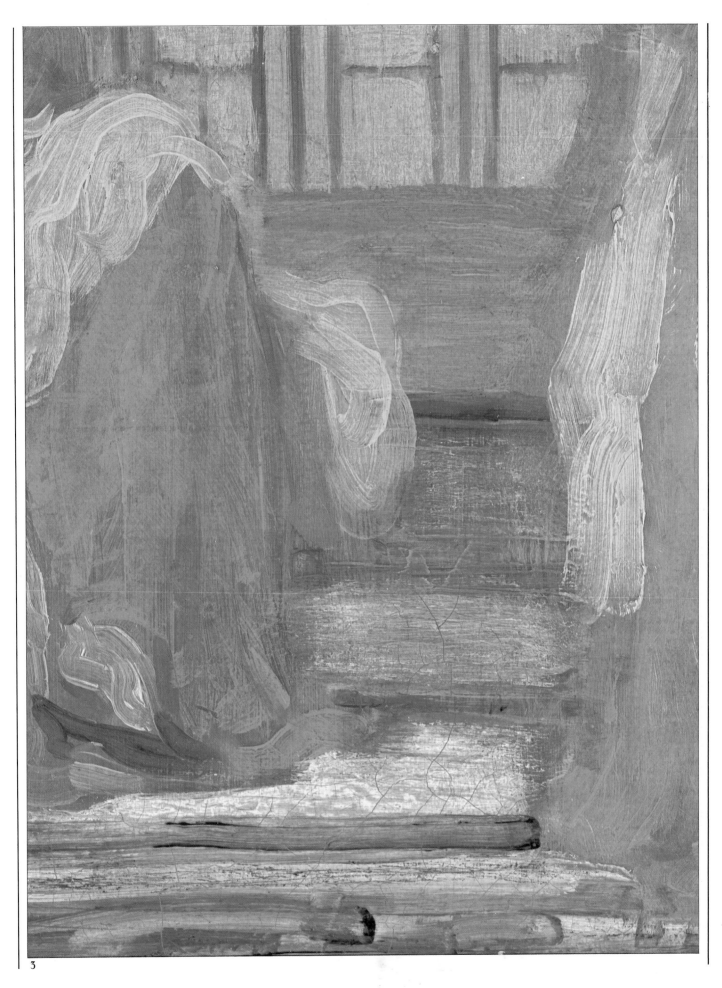

3

NOCTURNE IN BLUE AND GREEN: CHELSEA

1871
Oil on canvas
19³/₄×23¹/₂in/50×59.5cm
Tate Gallery, London

One of the earliest of Whistler's Nocturnes, this is a view across the Thames in London, seen from Battersea, with the tower of Old Chelsea Church in the distance. The exclusion of all inessential details, together with the almost monochromatic coloration, make it a typical example of the genre for which Whistler is today best remembered. The base colors were swept in over a dark ground and, as usual in Whistler's work, the details of the Japanese-inspired boatman, barge and butterfly signature were added later with sinuous ribbons of paint. Every element of the picture's composition is balanced against one against the other to create an exquisite and harmonious design that, like a piece of music, appeals directly to our senses.

Whistler had a special love of the twilight, which he saw as perhaps the only time when nature approached his own high standards of aesthetic perfection. He described his feelings in his famous *10 o'clock Lecture* of 1888. "And when the evening mist clothes the riverside with poetry, as with a veil, and the poor buildings lose themselves in the sky, and the tall chimneys become *campanili*, and the warehouses are palaces in the night, and the whole city hangs in the heavens, and fairyland is before us . . . Nature, who, for once has sung in tune, sings her exquisite song to the artist alone . . ."

"I can't thank you too much," he wrote to his friend and patron, the shipping magnate, Sir Francis Leyland, "for the name Nocturne as the title for my Moonlights. You, have no idea what an irritation it proves to my critics, and consequent pleasure to me, besides it is really so charming, and does so poetically say all I want to say and no more than I wish."

Despite the originality of his own art, Whistler made it clear in the closing remarks of his lecture that he saw the artist's task as one of continuing what had gone before, not searching for some unique style for the mere sake of novelty. "We have then but to wait — until, with the mark of the Gods upon him — there come among us again the chosen — who shall continue what has gone on before. Satisfied that, even were he never to appear, the story of the beautiful is already complete — hewn in the marbles of the Parthenon — and broidered, with the birds, upon the fan of Hokusai — at the foot of Fujiyama."

The lithographer T. R. Way has described Whistler's idiosyncratic manner of producing his wonderfully evocative works. ". . . Pointing to a group of buildings in the distance, an old public house at the corner of the road, with windows and shops showing golden lights through the gathering mist of the twilight, he said, 'Look!' As he did not seem to have anything to sketch or make notes on, I offered him my note-book, 'No, no, be quiet,' was the answer; and after a long pause he turned and walked back a few yards; then with his back turned to the scene at which I was looking, he said, 'Now see if I have learned it,' and repeated a full description of the scene, even as one might repeat a poem one had learned by heart."

Thus the elaborate paraphernalia of actuality would be reduced to its essential characteristics, those that had initially caught the artist's imagination. This distillation would then be used as the model for the subsequent painting, which was produced, not before the subject itself, vainly attempting to capture a fugitive effect, but in the confines of the studio, working from memory and the imagination. As Whistler saw it, mundane reality was to be studied only in order to be transformed by the temperament or vision of the artist into a thing of flawless beauty and universal significance.

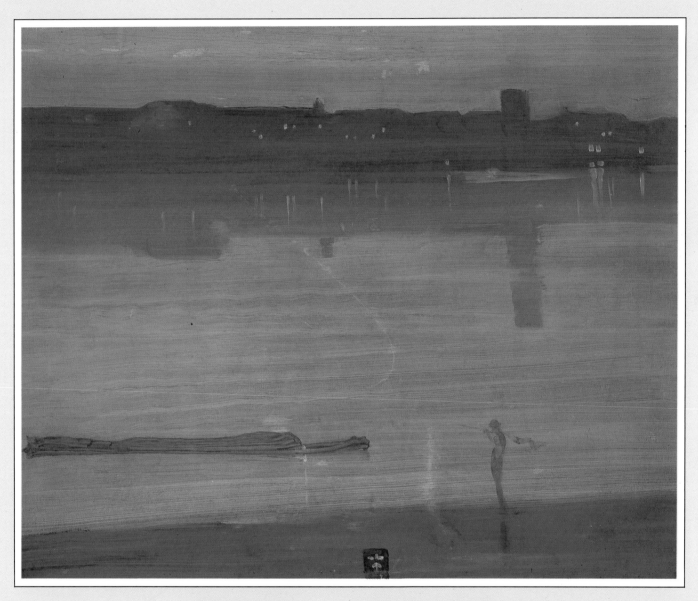

Few other of Whistler's paintings so perfectly illustrate the belief he expressed in his *10 o'clock Lecture.* "Nature contains the elements, in color and form, of all pictures ... But the artist is born to pick and choose, and group with science, these elements, that the result may be beautiful — as the musician gathers his notes ... To say to the painter, that Nature is to be taken as she is, is to say to the player, that he may sit at the piano."

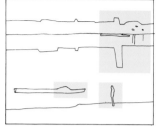

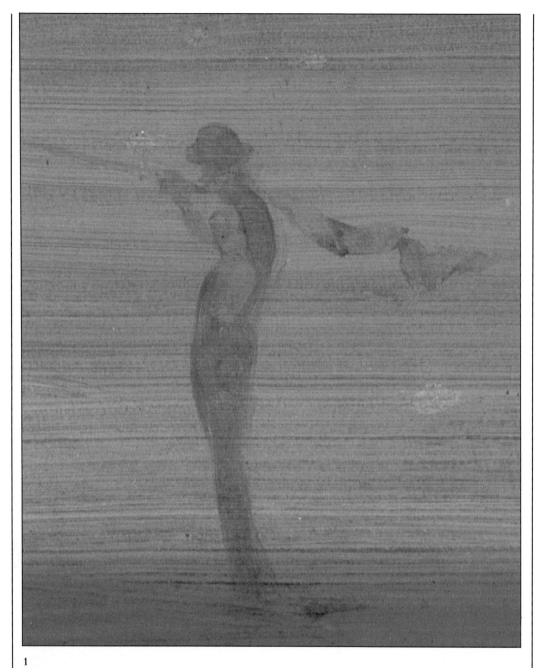

1

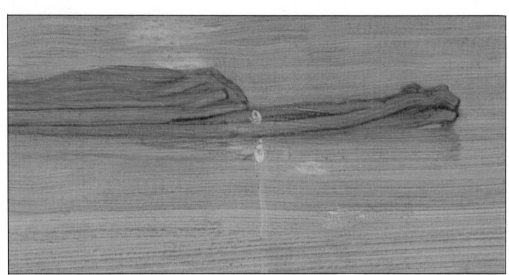

2

1 A single figure as delicate and decoratively imagined as one on a piece of Chinese porcelain stands on the shore, marking the asymmetry of the major compositional elements. The figure, like the cartouche, reiterates the decorative nature of the painting and shows the influence of the Japanese habit of making signatures part of the overall design of a picture.

2 The composition is founded on bands of subtly modulated color, shifting from blue-grey to blue-green. Simple block-like shapes are played off against dots and dashes of gradated yellow tones.

3 *Actual size details* The paint is swept on in broad swathes, with the brush taken from one edge of the canvas to the other. Nothing is centrally placed; the pictorial elements weave around the central spread of water. The thin paint leaves the trace of brushmarks in places, contrasting with more broadly handled areas from which the forms appear to emerge. Like Monet's paintings, this work hovers between the figurative and the abstract and, also like Monet, it captures perfectly the subdued luminosity and all-enveloping atmosphere characteristic of twilight.

3 *Actual size detail*

HARMONY IN GRAY AND GREEN:
MISS CICELY ALEXANDER

1872-3

Oil on canvas

74¾×38½in/189.9×97.8cm

Tate Gallery, London

This painting could easily be retitled "Homage to Velasquez." This banker's daughter, like one of the Spanish painter's young *infantas,* looks out of the canvas with an air of haughty disdain. Or could it be merely the discomfort and boredom she felt after having endured a reputed seventy or so sittings? Her pose, too, is reminiscent of Velasquez, although it was actually taken from the little boy holding the censer in Courbet's *Burial at Ornans* of 1850. The whiteness of the boy's robe is here exchanged for a white dress of Whistler's own design, which was specially starched by his mother to make the frills and skirt stand out.

The sitter later described the sessions to Whistler's biographers Joseph and Elizabeth Pennell (*The Life of James McNeill Whistler,* 1908). "I'm afraid I rather considered that I was a victim all through the sittings, or rather standings, for he never let me change my position, and I believe I used to get very tired and cross and often ended the day in tears . . . [he] never noticed the tears; he used to stand a good way from his canvas, and then dart at it, and then dart back, and he often turned around to look in a looking-glass that hung over the mantelpiece at his back — I suppose to see the reflection of his painting . . ."

While Whistler was painting this portrait he was also working on one of Carlyle (see page 51), and the story is told of a meeting between "the old man coming out and the little girl going in, 'Who is that?' he asked the maid. 'Miss Alexander, who was sitting to Mr Whistler,' he was told. Carlyle shook his head, 'Puir lassie! Puir lassie!' and, without another word, he went out."

The ground of the painting is dark brown, and the transparency of the dress was formed by the continual rubbing down of previous attempts to paint the skirt until several carefully judged touches of the brush delivered the desired effect. Writing of another portrait of the same period, the Pennells give us an interesting insight into the artist's working methods. "Whistler carried out his method of putting in the whole picture at once. The background was as much part of the design as the face. If anything went wrong anywhere the whole picture had to come out and be started again . . . the system taught by Gleyre, and developed in the Nocturnes was perfected in the portraits . . . The tones, made from a very few colors of infinite gradations, were mixed on the great palette, with black as the basis." The "great palette" is a reference to the three-foot-long polished mahogany table Whistler used instead of a palette when working on large oils. He prepared the painting on this, tone for tone, the final painting being an exact counterpart to his unorthodox palette, and he would spend as much time on this stage as on the canvas itself. At the end of a portrait sitting the painting was either declared finished or it was washed down with spirits in preparation for a fresh start the following session — usually the latter. Gradually over the twenty or so sittings that were the norm for a full-length portrait, a ghostly image of the sitter would appear, its presence enriching the final touches of paint. When successful, as in this work, the result has a marvelous freshness and unity of surface.

When the art critic of *The Times* saw this portrait he remarked that the upright line in the paneling of the wall was wrong, and the picture would be better without it, adding, "Of course it's only a matter of taste." To which Whistler replied, "I thought that perhaps for once, you were going to get away without having said something foolish; but remember, so that you may not make the same mistake again, it's not a matter of taste at all, it is a matter of knowledge. Goodbye."

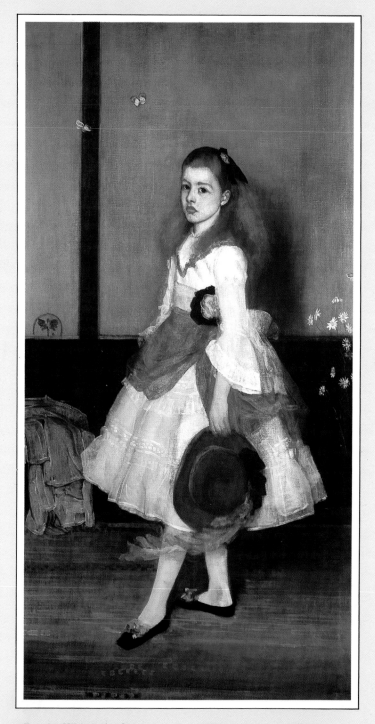

Despite Whistler's often-repeated assertions to the contrary, his successful portraits are often visual documents of great psychological insight. It is hard to see this painting as nothing more than an arrangement of tones and colors, although it certainly displays the artist's powers as a creator of exquisitely balanced formal inventions. Many of the most solid-looking areas of his mature works reveal the texture and color of the canvas ground beneath, which has the effect of subtly modifying the tonal values of the painting and thereby adding a further unifying effect to the composition. Whistler always strove to create above all an aura of harmony and restraint.

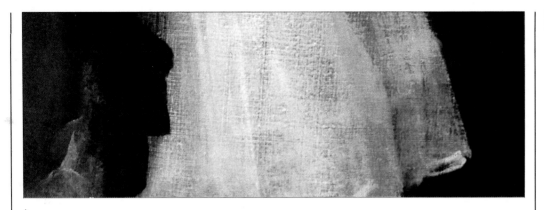

1

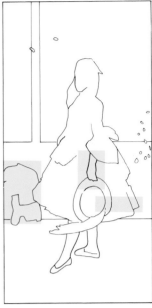

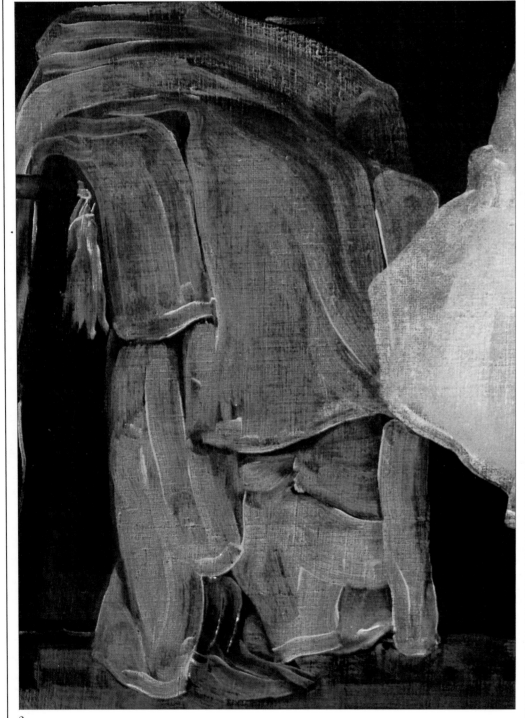

2

1 The painting is the result of a series of superimposed layers of excessively thin paint washed over a dark ground. This technique was particularly effective for rendering the semi-transparent white muslin, which only partially obscures the sitter's form. The black of the dado area can be clearly seen, modified by the various layers of paint which describe the dress and petticoat. If Whistler was dissatisfied with the painting at the end of a sitting, the day's work would be scraped down or mopped in order to allow him to begin afresh the next day. In this way he could impart to the final image a sense of freshness and immediacy which belied the labor that went into its creation.

2 This detail is a testimony to Whistler's ability to use paint descriptively in rapid gestural movements. Here he uses the minimum of brushstrokes to convey the weight of the sitter's coat as it hangs over a stool. The structure of the fabric is suggested by the thinness and transparency of the applied color modified by the presence of the dark underpainting.

3 *Actual size detail* Traces of the previous positioning of the sitter's arm can be clearly seen in this detail.

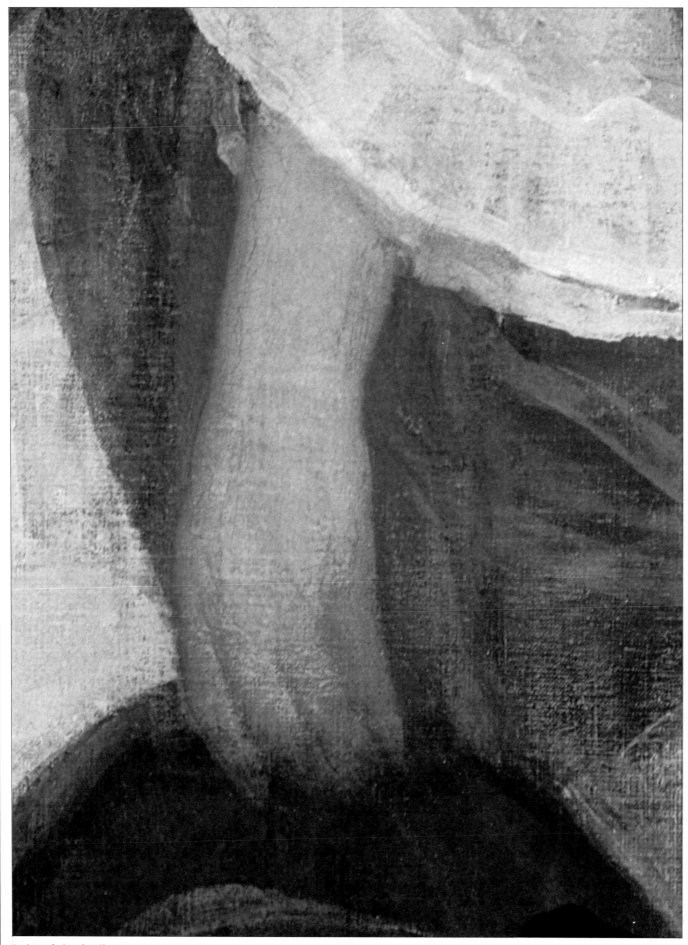

3 *Actual size detail*

ARRANGEMENT IN GRAY AND BLACK No. 2: THOMAS CARLYLE

1872-73
Oil on canvas
67⅜ × 56½ in / 171 × 143.5cm
Glasgow Art Gallery

Carlyle had admired Whistler's *Portrait of the Artist's Mother* (now in the Musée d'Orsay, Paris), and had reluctantly given the artist permission to paint his own. He was soon to regret it. One of Whistler's friends recalled something of the suffering to which Whistler's sitters were subjected. "If Carlyle makes signs of moving his position, Whistler screams out in an agonized tone, 'For God's sake don't move!' Carlyle said afterwards that all Whistler's anxiety seemed to be to get the *coat* painted to ideal perfection: the face went for little. He had begun by asking for one or two sittings, but managed to get a great many. At last Carlyle flatly rebeled. He used to define Whistler as the most absurd creature on the face of the earth."

The painting is modelled upon Velasquez, but it is a mark of its success that no one particular painting by the Spanish master springs to mind. Whistler claimed that he was uninterested in producing a psychological reading of his sitter's personality, but was concerned only with the pictorial organization of certain lines, shapes and colors to create an aesthetically pleasing design.

Like the paintings of the Dutch masters he admired so much, Whistler has created a picture which gives the impression of having been painted "with a single skin." In other words, as Whistler used to say, the canvas has not been "embarrassed" or over-fussed; his concern was always to ensure that the final image revealed no trace of the anguished work that went into its creation. The Irish writer George Moore remarked that the paint which describes the head of the sitter "often hardly amounts to more than a glaze, and painting is laid over painting, like skin upon a skin." Ghostly shadows surrounding the rakish silhouette of the great philosopher mark the artist's previous decisions as to the size and shape of the sitter's figure, the position of the hand holding the cane and the fall of his coat. Even the position and type of chair was modified several times. The polarities of the tonal range are carefully stated in the crisp white of Carlyle's stiffly starched collar and the dense black of his hat, which is set at an exactly measured angle to repeat in reverse the contour formed by the sitter's torso. The subtlety of the tones and the breaking of the strictly geometrical organization of the picture surface is evident in the positioning of Carlyle's hat so that it neatly obscures the lower right-hand corner of a picture frame. The effect of extreme simplicity is the result of Whistler's carefully contrived art.

Ironically, Whistler has often been criticized for his apparently haphazard manner of working, but in fact the care he took with his paintings borders on the fanatical, and a close examination of this picture reveals him as a master of control and economy of means. He has used brushes of a surprising breadth: a ½-in (1.25cm) brush describes both the sitter's hair and the artist's butterfly signature; while the thin paint of the outlined black cloak was swept on with a 1¼-in (3cm) brush. The pigment used in the picture was so dilute that it is possible to see where it has dripped.

Despite all Whistler's claims to the contrary, the portrait evokes an extraordinarily powerful sympathy for the sitter, whose meditative and melancholy gaze beyond the physical limits of the canvas recalls his earlier portraits. He wrote to a friend in 1891, "He is a favorite of mine. I like the gentle sadness about him! — perhaps he was sensitive — and even misunderstood — who knows!"

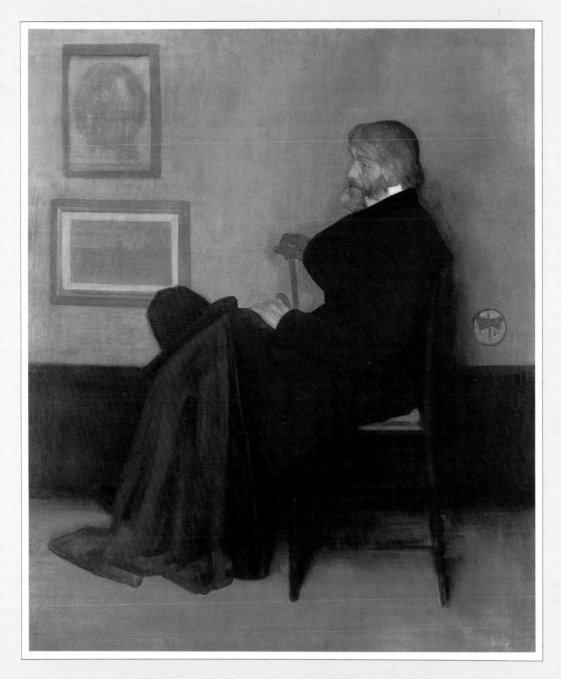

This portrait constitutes a visual document of Whistler's love of Classical and Japanese art and the work of Velasquez, as well as demonstrating his own finely tuned powers of perception. The delicate silvery gray of the sitter's hair and beard occupies the middle position on a wide tonal scale. This ranges from the densest of blacks at one end to the crispest of whites at the other. A cunning interplay of geometrical and near-geometrical shapes sets up a sophisticated series of asymmetrical relationships across the canvas surface.

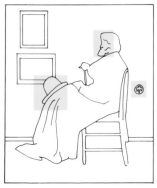

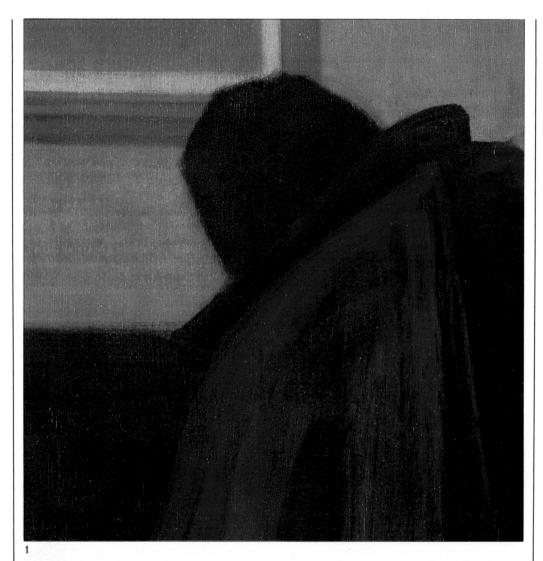

1

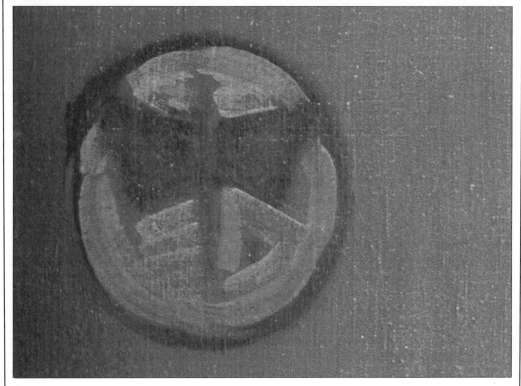

2

1 The gray used to describe Carlyle's coat has been used in such a dilute form that several traces of dripped paint are visible. Whistler used what he described as his "sauce" so thinly that is has been absorbed by the canvas, giving the impression that the design is not resting on top of the canvas, but is an integral part of it. Among the many delights of Whistler's paintings is the beauty of their matt surface texture. He disliked paint that looked overworked or "embarrassed."

2 The butterfly emblem is robustly painted with the block-like strokes of a ½ in (1.2cm) paint brush. The vigor of these strokes contrasts with the restraint of handling evident in the rest of the picture.

3 *Actual size detail* The necessity of describing the sitter's powerful features could easily have spoiled the harmonious effect that Whistler always sought. He has used a carefully controlled technique in painting the head. Tone lies next to tone in simple flat areas of paint, building up an exquisite mosaic of planes that describe Carlyle's melancholy face while respecting the flatness of the canvas surface.

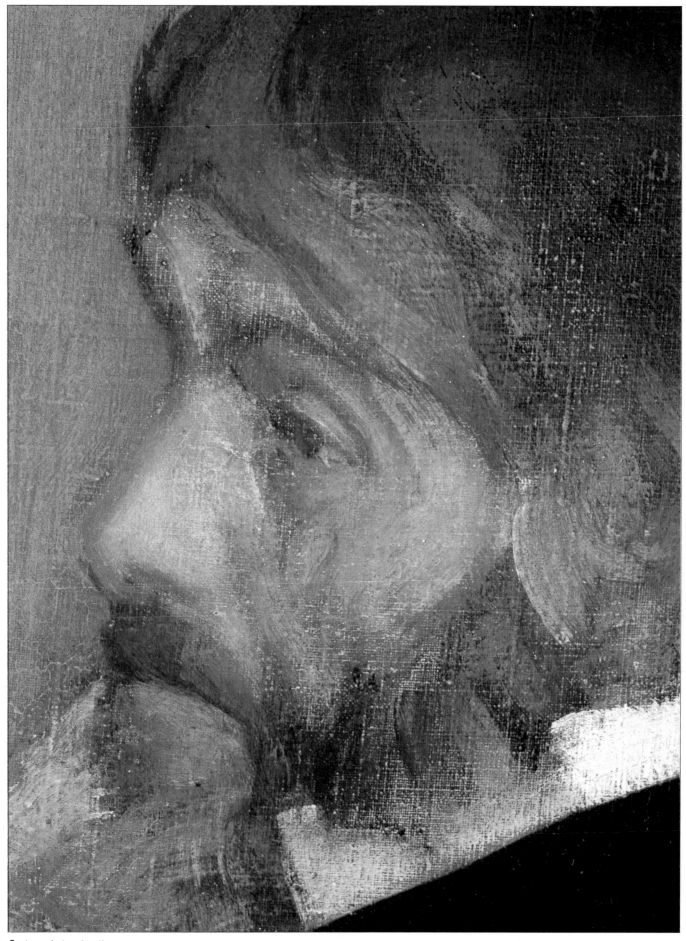

3 *Actual size detail*

Nocturne in Black and Gold: the Falling Rocket

c1875
Oil on wood
23¾×18⅛in/60.3×46.6cm
Detroit Institute of Arts

This is one of Whistler's most dramatic and effective canvases, painted with a freedom and verve unusual in both his art and that of his contemporaries. When it was exhibited at the Grosvenor Gallery in 1877 it attracted the attention — and wrath — of the elderly art critic John Ruskin. He considered the price of 200 guineas for "flinging a pot of paint in the face of the public" a gross impertinence, and said so in his review. The point in question was whether the time that the artist had spent on a painting was reflected in its monetary value. Ruskin felt that the public was not being given value for money, and was duty bound to say so. Whistler, not only quarrelsome by nature, but also worried at the potential damage to his status as a portrait painter, sued the critic, and although the technical winner of the case, was made to pay costs, which is the legal way of saying that the case should not have been brought. The trial was a farce. Ruskin was too ill to attend, and Whistler's friend Burne-Jones, who appeared against his will to help Whistler, at one point made an unintentional indictment of the artist's work by saying that he ". . . evaded the difficulties of painting by not carrying his work far enough." "This," said *The Times* in its leader of November 27, "would probably be accepted as a fair representation of the truth by everybody." The trial bankrupted Whistler but ensured the painting's place in history.

The Grosvenor Gallery, which was made gentle fun of in Gilbert and Sullivan's operetta *Patience,* was opened as an alternative to the over-commercialized Royal Academy. Whistler exhibited eight works there in the company of Burne-Jones, Rossetti and others associated with the Aesthetic movement. In court Whistler was asked to describe the painting which had caused such offense. "The picture represents a distant view of Cremorne, with a falling rocket and other fireworks. It occupied two days and is a finished picture. The frame is traced with black, and the black mark on the right is my monogram. What is the particular beauty of the picture? I dare say I could make it clear to any sympathetic painter, but I do not think that I could to you [i.e. the Attorney-General], any more than a musician could explain the beauty of a harmony to a person who had no ear."

William Rossetti, the critic and brother of Dante Gabriel Rossetti, wrote of the picture, "The scene is probably Cremorne Gardens; the heavy rich darkness of the clump of the trees to the left, contrasted with the opaque obscurity of the sky, itself enhanced by the falling shower of fire-flakes, is felt and realized with great truth. Straight across the trees, not high above the ground, shoots and fizzles the last and fiercest light of the expiring rocket." Whistler may well have been helped in visualizing this scene by the print of a similar subject by the Japanese artist Hiroshige, but the major means which enabled him to translate the scene so directly was his technique of memorizing experience so thoroughly that he could recall its essentials later in the quiet of his studio.

The ground is reddish brown, which gives a warm glow to the blue-black of the night sky. The particular milky quality of the sky is the result of Whistler's method of introducing transparent blue-gray washes into the painting. The general thinness of the paint enhances the thickly impasted horizontal strokes of yellow-red that establish the setting of the display and help to define the architectural details half hinted at in the middle distance. The fireworks are brilliantly described by firmly placed dabs of orange and green, which stand out in dramatic contrast with the rest of the painting. The figures are established by the color of the background rather than by any direct application of paint, their flat, modish silhouettes once again bringing Japan to mind, quite appropriately, given the subject of the painting.

Because this painting initially achieved fame through the infamous court case between Whistler and Ruskin, its artistic qualities are sometimes under-appreciated. As with so many of Whistler's paintings, its beauty lies not only in the formal inventions and the painterly innovations, but also in the courage of the artist in breaking new ground. Whistler and other avant-garde artists of the late 19th rcentury were engaged in a similar struggle to develop new and more truthful ways of recording their sensations before an ever-changing nature.

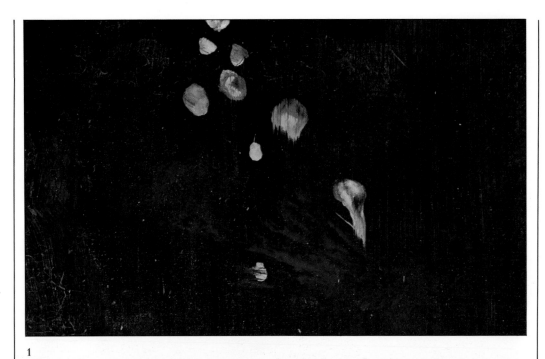

1

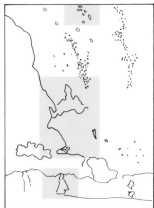

1 Details of this painting reveal the extent to which Whistler abstracted from nature. Here one can almost feel the twists and turns of his wrist as he placed the varied dots and dashes that describe the sparks thrown off by the exploding fireworks, blazing with light as they tumble down to earth.

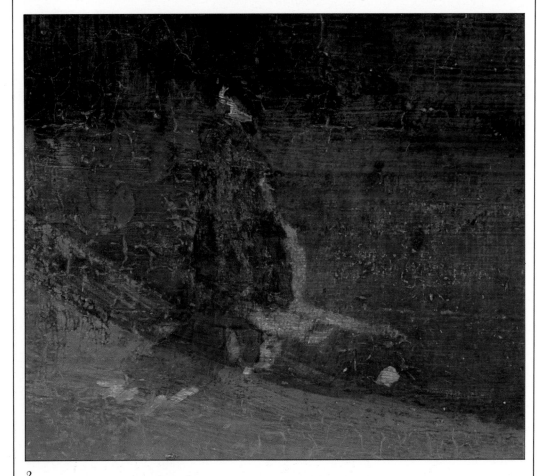

2

2 The painting was done on a red-brown ground, and the only color of the foreground figure is that of this underpainting. When the Attorney General was told at the trial that the picture had probably taken "one day to do the work and another to finish," he asked whether "that is the labor for which you asked 200 guineas?" The artist replied, "No, it was for the knowledge of a lifetime."

3 *Actual size detail* A vivid horizontal flash of impasted yellow paint moves across the picture, losing itself in the darkness only to reappear as a parti-colored blob of red-yellow. This is repeated in the bands of yellow lights that mark the verticals of the fantastical buildings of the Pleasure Gardens, which, by their very regularity, contrast with the flecks of paint that describe the falling sparks. Paint has been washed on and dabbed out to create the impression of mystery inherent in such a scene, brilliantly but sporadically lit by short-lived flashes of color.

3 *Actual size detail*

BATHING POSTS, BRITTANY

1893
Oil on wood
6½×9½in/16.6×24.5cm
Hunterian Museum and Art Gallery, University of Glasgow

Water had always fascinated Whistler, and in the 1880s he began to produce a series of paintings *en plein air* — directly studied from nature — which are very different from either his earlier Courbet-inspired canvases or his near-monochromatic Nocturnes. These tiny panels were produced with the aid of a small box of oils, which contained panels of wood cut just large enough to fit inside the box itself.

For an artist who is most often remembered for his skill in balancing nuances of grays and blues, silvers and opals, these small panels are surprising in the exactitude with which they capture the kind of light and color revealed by full daylight. From his earliest paintings Whistler had preferred to situate himself so that the subject of his composition was fixed in terms of a series of horizontal and/or vertical accents that echoed the sides of his support, in this case, the rectangular shape of his panel. This served both to reduce the problems of perspective and to allow his flat areas of subtly modulated color to give maximum assistance to his intention, namely to create a formal balance made up of a few simple geometrically based forms.

Here he has produced such a formal arrangement, and in some of his late paintings he was to push this trend even further, paring away all detail until all that remained was a series of horizontal bands. These, by their tone and color, are made to suggest with the utmost economy of means the vastness of the sea and sky.

Here the long, delicately drawn lines of thin paint cover the panel from side to side, the broad description of the scene being created by no more than the pressure of the artist's hand and the gradual emptying of his brush, while a few flicks of muted color and carefully placed triangles of white serve as the small details that complete the illusion of

actuality. In their somewhat over-fulsome biography of the artist, the Pennells described his procedure. "When the wave broke and the surf made a beautiful line of white, he painted this at once, then all that completed the beauty of the breaking wave, then the boat passing, and then, having got the movement and the beauty that goes almost as soon as it comes, he put in the shore or the horizon."

Paintings like this one reveal a carefree desire to paint with freedom and lack of inhibition that could only with great difficulty have been achieved in the larger and more carefully planned pictures of the artist's earlier career. Working on a small scale directly from his unpretentious subject matter imposed technical limitations that gave him new scope for improvisation, and the enjoyment he clearly felt in producing these works has an impact that belies their physical size. Whistler called these tiny miracles of painting his "little games," and their rigorous, if unassuming geometry and controlled application of color and tone make them some of the most delightful of all his productions. Sickert observed that "Whistler expressed the essence of his talent in his little panels — *pochades,* it is true, in measurement, but masterpieces of classic painting in importance." The modest size of these *pochades* (sketches or studies), whether they depict a row of shops, a seascape or group of humble farm buildings, allowed the artist to sidestep many of the problems he confronted in larger projects and to express some of the concerns that he found so difficult to give voice to in other, perhaps more taxing, undertakings. In a letter to the Pennells towards the end of his life he said, "I could almost laugh at the extraordinary progress I am making and the lovely things I am inventing — work beyond anything I have ever done before."

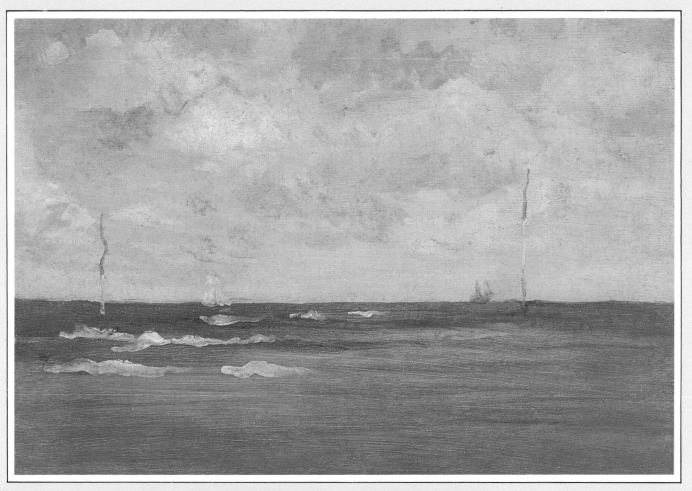

The panel is divided horizontally into almost equal portions, each of which has been painted quite differently. This tiny seascape could easily be mistaken for a detail from a larger work by one of the Impressionists, although the techniques employed are very different. However, the thinness of the medium and fluidity of handling in the picture recalls the seascape in the background of Degas' painting, *On the Beach* (National Gallery, London), which may well have owed something to Whistler's paintings of the 1860s.

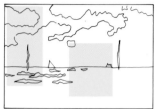

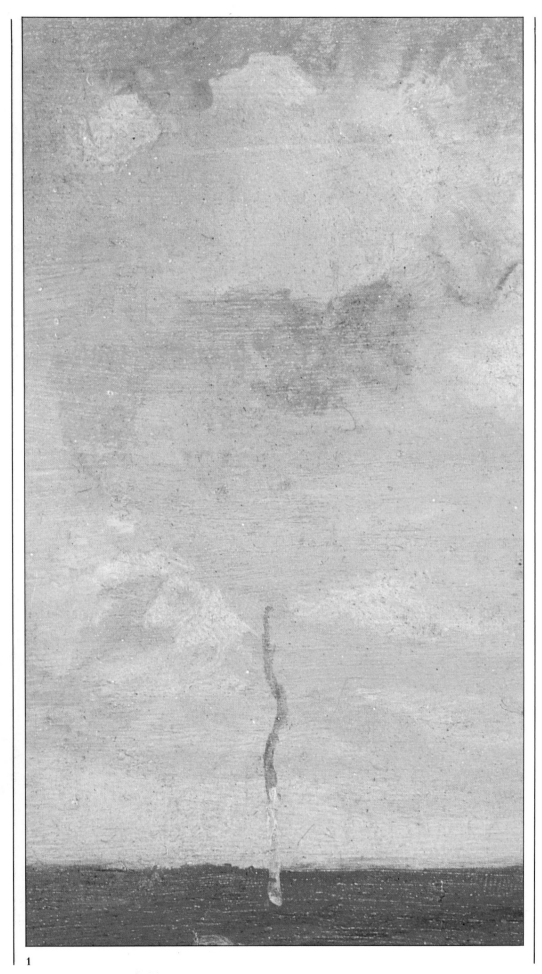

1 Ultramarine mixed with white is dabbed in single brushmarks on a gray ground in a manner traditionally associated with watercolor, leaving the ground to show through to suggest the color and form of the clouds. The structure of the clouds is tightened by the addition of a richer mixture of the ground color. The far distance is suggested by a thin wash of pinkish lilac which brings out the delicate colors of the bathing posts.

2 The sea is described with a translucent wash of paint that appears to have been wiped to suggest the gentle movement of waves. Where it recedes into the distance the paint has been left undisturbed, its stronger color indicating the broader, flatter expanse. The series of waves have been brushed on and then taken off with the brush, allowing the grain of the wood to show through to suggest the darker undersides, while single perfectly controlled dabs of paint describe the white tops of the breakers.

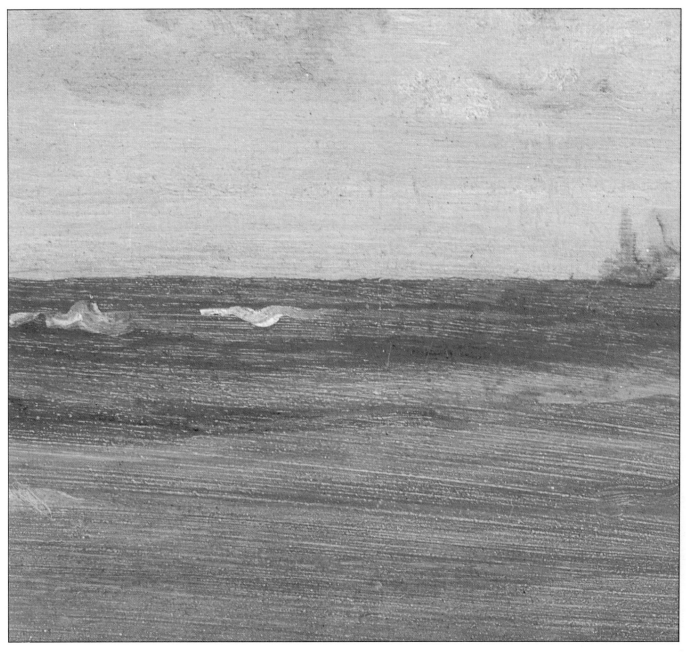

2

INDEX

ACKNOWLEDGEMENTS

PHOTOGRAPHIC CREDITS

Detroit Institute of Arts 6, 10, 55-57; Freer Gallery of Art, Washington 11, 14 top, 19-21, 35-37; Glasgow Art Gallery 51-53; Hunterian Museum and Art Gallery, University of Glasgow 12, 15, 59-61; Manchester City Art Gallery 9 bottom; Municipal Gallery of Modern Art, Dublin 8; Museum of Fine Arts, Boston 39-41; National Gallery of Art, Washington 7, 23-25; National Gallery of Scotland, Edinburgh 9 top; Prado, Madrid 14 bottom; Tate Gallery, London 27-29, 31-33, 43-45, 47-49.